The Bleus Br

By

Mike Pearce

Acknowledgements

There are a lot of people who have helped me throughout the process of getting this book written and published, and I dedicate it to them.

To my dear friend and literary hero Stephen Jones who supported me, as he has always done since the start of my journalistic career, I cannot buy you enough pastries to thank you, but I'm sure you will let me try.

To my wife Liz and the kids, Emily and Jamie, who have grown up so wonderfully, thank you for your love and support, both the moral and technical kind, and to my four-legged friend Rufus, the black lab, he was by my side constantly while I would hammer away at the keyboard, and regularly thrust an empty plastic water bottle into my crotch to keep me focused and to obtain yet another charcoal bone. Ruf, you are the best friend a man could ever have.

It would be remiss of me not to mention my dear son-in-law, Kader, who educated me like a kung Fu master on the vagaries and complexities of the French male psyche, merci for your friendship, your love and for the use of your Lavazza machine though not necessarily in that order.

To Mam and Dad, I still can't really believe you've gone. I know you'd have been amazed to discover that I had actually read a book, let alone written one, but here it is. I only wish you were still here to share this moment with me. Thank you for all the *Rugby World* magazines you bought me during my childhood, for nurturing my love of this wonderful game and most importantly for making me Welsh.

Thanks to my friends Phil Steele, Jonathan Davies ('Jiffy'), former World Rugby CEO Brett Gosper and Scottish International Debs McCormack for their thoughts, memories and support.

To those wonderful rugby players Emile, Aurélien, Mathieu, the two Philippes. Yoann, Franck, Pascal, Guilhem, Gérard, Walter, Seb, Jean-Pierre, Serge and Marc, without you this book would not have been possible, merci.

Last, but very definitely not least, a huge thank you to my friend, Carmarthenshire farmer and referee Nigel Owens. A truly amazing man whom I am honoured and privileged to count as a friend. Thanks for offering to write the foreword to this book with such grace and enthusiasm; you are one in a million, Diolch.

Prologue

I've been racking my brains to recall the exact date or moment when my love affair with French rugby actually started. Despite my best efforts, I can't pin it down, but I do know that it was sometime in the 1970s.

As a young boy from west Wales, like everyone else in my part of the world, I was seduced by my country's Grand Slam-winning superstars, and I was only really interested in my red-shirted heroes, the ones who played at nearby Stradey Park for Llanelli and the ones who played for Wales.

My heroes had superfluous surnames; they were known to all and sundry by their first names or nicknames while some of the very special ones only required initials.

Gareth, Barry, Gerald, Swerve, Benny, J. J. and J. P. R.; they and their teammates filled all my hopes and dreams.

Then one day, and I have no idea when it occurred, I discovered another rugby world. It was a world that encompassed all the beauty and brutality I already knew, but one that was accompanied by a touch of some indefinable elegance and élan plus a touch of brutality.

That game was played in sunshine, a rare and mystical commodity where I came from. Its backs played with their collars turned up; they charmed me with angles of running that defied Pythagoras and they did things with the ball that I had never seen before. Many of them resembled film stars more than rugby players.

The forwards were terrifying; they looked like they had been hewn from the rocks of the Pyrenees but even so they had a sort of industrial beauty amid their beastliness.

Rugby of course in those far off days was a world away from today's professional fare. There were no television cameras prying into every scrum, ruck and maul and it was a bit like the Wild West.

If France pushed the boundaries in joyous silky back play, they also did so in the execution of the dark arts. The players that perpetrated these acts are too numerous to mention but this book has managed to capture a few of them.

In recent years I've spent a lot of time covering French rugby and have been fortunate enough to meet some wonderful people. I even ended up accompanying Bernard Laporte on the piano on the day France were awarded the 2023 Rugby World Cup. Laporte and Chabal on vocals and me on keyboards – that was some "Boy Band". ("Boise bande" in French a native speaker advises me.) But as the wine flowed our tempo slowed and we began to resemble a Gallic version of Flanders and Swann.

Charles de Gaulle once famously declared: "How can you govern a country that has 246 varieties of cheese?" The diversity of France (its landscape, climate and people) is also truly reflected in its rugby.

Ancient rivalries and feuds echo across the chapters of this book, many of which have absolutely nothing to do with the game.

One of the most emotive and explosive topics of discussion in this beautiful country is the eternal battle over the naming rights of a particular pastry item.

Forget the Basque-Catalan derby match between Bayonne and Perpignan, the pain au chocolat vs the chocolatine is one battle that is always a tasty affair in every sense.

This particular pastry is called a chocolatine in south-west France but known as a pain au chocolat everywhere else. People from Bordeaux actually boycotted the pain au chocolat and it was common to find a chocolatine for €1 next to a pain au chocolat for €1.50 in the same bakery.

In 2018, President Macron was lobbied to get the term "chocolatine" a reserved spot in the French dictionary. The President mentioned the debate in a speech, and everything escalated until it reached Parliament.

MPs (députés) fought for "chocolatine" to be acknowledged as an official term. They wanted the pastry to keep its fame and status through its name.

Leaving pastries to one side, rugby is a religion in the deep south-west of France, a passion that has expressed and fueled village and small-town rivalries in the region for over a century. Draw a line roughly from Bordeaux to Marseilles, and another along the ridge of the Pyrenees from the Atlantic to the Mediterranean, and you enclose the ancient provinces of Gascony and Languedoc and the parts of France that are Basque and Catalan. You have also defined the boundaries of what many call simply "l'Ovalie", the Land of the Oval Ball.

Heading north there are the city slickers of Paris, regarded with deep suspicion and disdain by their southern opponents, Stade Français and Racing 92 with their money and their airs and graces not being looked upon favourably.

Yet even in Paris parochialism is rife; Racing 92 – until they recently moved to their space age stadium in La Defense – played at Colombes and were deeply offended if anyone referred to them as a Parisian outfit. For the record, Colombes is a six-minute Métro journey away from the centre of the capital.

So French rugby is about far more than the 80 minutes on the field, and the one thing that unites everyone from the bronzed Basques to the pasty Parisians is their differences on and off the field. Vive la difference!

I trust this book celebrates them and their pastries in a fitting manner.

Mike Pearce

Trug Cottage

East Sussex

Foreword

When Mike approached me to write a foreword for his book I didn't hesitate to say yes.

I first met Mike after a talk I did in central London a few years ago, and then through our friendship I became aware of his writing when I started reading his weekly website column the "Monday Roar".

His passion for rugby and particularly French rugby is evident in his writing.

His enjoyable articles always give an insight into the matches, characters and history of the game which I have a particular appetite for.

This book on French rugby gives an insight into some of the greats of the game. It also gives a colourful back story of French culture, cuisine and history.

There is something special about standing in the middle of the Stade de France while 80,000 people belt out La Marseillaise. I have been fortunate to experience that stirring anthem not only in Paris but also Lyon, Montpellier and even Marseille itself.

Having spent a large part of my rugby career in France, refereeing at European cup and international matches, I have seen first-hand just how much the French value their rugby history and heritage.

The French, like the Welsh, are a passionate people and particularly when it comes to rugby.

Sometimes that passion can spill over, as indeed it did when I refereed a match between Perpignan and Leeds. The match was decided by a retaken conversion that gave Leeds victory. After the game, the Perpignan coach kicked open my changing room door and starting shouting at me in French. I had a pretty good idea as to what he was saying.

I've been privileged to referee *Les Bleus* on many occasions. The first time was in the 2008 Six Nations when France lost to Ireland 21-26 in Paris.

I also refereed the England vs France game at Twickenham on Super Saturday in the 2015 Six Nations, the final match that rounded off one of the best days of international rugby. It was a match that will live long in the memory with the French turning on some brilliance in a pulsating game.

The Wales vs France matches were always something special when I was young and were invariably the matches that decided the Five Nations Championship. I saw a lot of these games; they were brilliant and exciting in equal measure.

I watched many of the players in this book while growing up and have also refereed a few of them. When you referee the French, you never know which team will turn up on any given day. They can be at their brilliant best or equally, below par.

One thing you can be sure of is that this book will be an exciting and brilliant read, just like the best of the French teams on their day.

Nigel Owens MBE

Mynyddcerrig

Sir Gaerfyrddin / Carmarthenshire

Chapter 1

Pascal Ondarts
"Those props are as cunning as a bag o' weasels."
Bill McLaren

"France Prop, Pascal Ondarts. Occupation: folk singer."
These were the words on a media release providing a pen
picture of the big Basque prop during the 1991 Rugby
World Cup, certainly one of the more unusual day jobs
during rugby's amateur era but not the most unusual.

Gerard Bouguyon, Grenoble's French international in
the 1930s, was a physics professor while more recently,
lock Francis Haget earned a crust as a croupier in a Biarritz
casino. Grégoire Lascubé of Biarritz Olympique and SU
Agen opted to combine law enforcement with scrum
enforcement when he became a detective. It is true to say
that Ondarts was, and still is a folk singer, but to say that it
was his occupation is stretching artistic license somewhat.

Basques are said to ask themselves three questions every
day: who are we, where do we come from and where are
going for dinner tonight?

In Basque mythology, Basajaun is a spirit and guardian
of the woods and nature who also protects the flocks. When
a storm approaches, Basajaun roars to alert the shepherds
so they can take shelter with their animals. He also appears
as a farmer, blacksmith or miller.

Like Basajaun, Ondarts was once a blacksmith in
Bayonne and when you see his body shape up close, it
really does looks like he swallowed the anvil.

His distinctive Basque nose has been fractured on at
least five occasions which makes that already rugged

feature even more prominent, but I would hazard a guess that he caused more broken noses than he received.

The Basque language is spoken by around one million people in France and Spain. However, while it is recognized as an official language in Spain, it is not afforded the same recognition in France.

The language is still widely spoken in Bayonne, and as you move away from the coast and into the foothills of the Pyrenees, the language, culture and traditions are more evident.

France has had its fair share of Basques in the national jersey including the late Michel Celaya from Biarritz who captained the country to its first ever outright Five Nations title in 1961.

Other notables include a prop who kept Ondarts out of the French team, Pierre Dospital, back row forward Imanol Harinordoquy, Laurent Pardo the Bayonne winger and France lock and captain in the 2020 Six Nations, Charles Ollivon.

If you take a short stroll inland from the beach at Biarritz, with the sound of the Atlantic rollers still ringing in your ears, you will reach Place Georges Clemenceau where the bright red awnings and the white walls of Le Royalty Brasserie will greet you like an oasis.

The entrecôte steak in a Béarnaise sauce with homemade fries is a treat to the senses, and the man bringing this delightful fare to your table may look strangely familiar for this establishment is owned by none other than Pascal Ondarts himself.

The warm friendly welcome will be in stark contrast to the greetings received by those who encountered mine host in front-row battles throughout his rugby career.

Pascal was a one-club man spending his entire playing career with Biarritz Olympique. Having been born some 30 miles inland, in the tiny Basque commune of Méharin, for him the Pyrénées-Atlantiques have always been home.

Coming from a large family – he had four brothers and a twin sister – I would hazard a guess that he was one of the first to arrive at the meal table and one of the last to leave.

"When I was young, rugby was not that widespread in the region where I lived. In my village, Méharin, some people didn't even know I played international rugby. Out in the countryside no one played rugby, we all played pelota; it is still my favourite sport. If I have to choose between a good rugby match and a game of pelota, I prefer pelota."

"I also used to enjoy the traditional Basque strength tests. I lifted over 270 kilos and carried a cart around the course four times.

"Our generation worked like Trojans; we worked all the time on the farm, seven days a week. It was only when I married my wife, Mireille, that I discovered weekends and it was she who encouraged me to take up rugby."

I witnessed Pascal up close on quite a few occasions in Cardiff, Paris and Twickenham, and he was always going to be a shoo-in for my France team. He was a prop with buttocks the size of Bayonne hams. His low centre of gravity made it virtually impossible to bring him to ground and to do so was a bit like attempting to dismantle a garden shed. Squat and compact at 5ft 10in and 16 stone, his scrummaging prowess was legendary.

Pascal was no stranger to the dark arts and didn't just limit his execution of those talents to opposition forwards. Much against the front row code of conduct, he was not averse to punching backs as well as his own kind.

Chris Tynan, the Canadian scrum-half, discovered this to his cost during a Rugby World Cup warm-up match although as you would expect from any self-respecting number nine, Tynan gave as good as he got. In a moment of extreme bravery or foolishness, he went chasing after Ondarts to exact revenge. Fortunately for him, he was restrained before he could get within range, a move that may have saved the little scrum-half a whole heap of trouble.

Ondarts' warming-up techniques for international matches included head-butting teammates and walls. It's a big step up from Pilates and hamstring stretches!

One of the all-time greats of the front row, Jeff Probyn the former England prop, has vivid memories of his own England debut in Paris.

"In my first match for England against France I took four balls against the head and each time I got a punch from Ondarts. Fortunately, I was experienced and wise enough to realize what was coming so I managed to duck and most of the punches landed on the top of my head causing no damage."

As my coffee arrives in front of the setting sun at Le Royalty, it's hard to envisage the violence and horror that occurred 300 miles up the Atlantic coast in Nantes on 15th November 1986, the day Pascal Ondarts made his international debut for France against New Zealand, a game widely regarded as one of the most brutal international matches of all time.

It resulted in a famous win for France in a match riddled with errors from both teams. The score was 3-3 at half-time but two French tries in the second half, from Denis Charvet and Alain Lorieux, were enough to give the home side victory.

Had Philippe Bérot had his kicking boots on that day, the margin of victory would have been much greater.

Ondarts was instructed to play midweek for a Côte Basque side against New Zealand to put his hand up for international selection for the match in Nantes.

Despite a loss to the All Blacks, he more than held his own against a formidable front row consisting of McDowall, Fitzpatrick and Boroevich so his international place was confirmed a few days later.

It may have been a successful debut for Ondarts but for All Black legend and number eight, Wayne Shelford, it was a particularly challenging match. He found himself at the bottom of a ruck after 20 minutes, a French boot tore open his scrotum leaving a testicle hanging out. Shelford had it stitched up on the touchline with the whole grisly process being shown live on French television. He returned to the fray to be knocked out cold and have several teeth removed with a punch.

He recalls: "It was my second international, I lost three teeth when someone kicked me and then I had to go off in the third quarter with concussion. My right testicle was ripped out of my scrotum and 18 stitches were needed to put everything back together. It was a physical and mental disaster."

"After being concussed later, I can't really remember anything much, and don't really want to. I've never seen so much blood, cut heads, cut eyes, it was everywhere."

Another casualty, of which there were many, the New Zealand hooker Sean Fitzpatrick had 26 stitches after being on the wrong end of the boot of French lock Jean Condom.

Serge Blanco, the French full back, recalls: "Unusually, we didn't warm up on the pitch. We did it out of sight and we used some very strong words. Jacques Fouroux, our coach, spoke to us not about the shirt or the flag but about us, the group, what we stood for in relation to each other and our families."

"We always respected the Haka but this time we advanced towards it and almost ended up under the All Blacks' noses. It was a way of telling them today we are going to turn up."

"In Nantes it was we who attacked. A week earlier in the first Test in Toulouse we were timid. At kick-off we trampled all over Murray Pierce as he caught the ball and that set the tone for what was to follow."

To add an even more sinister element to proceedings, Jacques Mombet (the France team doctor between 1975 and 1995) alleged that the national team used amphetamines and not only for the New Zealand game but regularly.

He admitted players were not obliged to take them but were free to do so and would be given them with their pre-match meal.

Many of the All Blacks commented on how the French were up to their eyeballs during the match in Nantes and unrecognizable from the team they beat in Toulouse a week earlier. It is worth bearing in mind that the use of amphetamines was not forbidden in rugby at that time.

Pascal Ondarts denies these allegations strenuously; in fact, he sued French newspaper *L'Équipe* over his photo being used to headline an article on the matter.

"I remember at the time I even had to drive my own car to Nantes. We were all amateurs and then this glass maker writes that we are on drugs. I have children and grandchildren. I don't want them to come and see us and be told their grandfather is an ex-French international but he took drugs. This is very serious to try and wash away my honour."

New Zealand discreetly advised the International Rugby Board about their concerns and the board in turn spoke to the French Rugby Federation resulting in a ban on the use of amphetamines in rugby and setting the scene for anti-doping measures to come into force around the national team.

New Zealand wing John Kirwan said that France out-muscled and bullied the All Blacks in Nantes.

"The game was filthy, and I remember the French props running onto the pitch before kick-off with blood running down their foreheads."

The All Blacks were given a tough time on that tour. One All Black told me: "The French give you an interpreter who hardly speaks any English and a coach driver who is always getting lost. And this before you get the s**t kicked out of you on the paddock."

Ondarts was involved in another violent and controversial match in 1991 when he was alleged to have thrown a punch at New Zealand referee David Bishop after France were defeated by England in Paris in a tempestuous Rugby World Cup semi-final.

The Ondarts incident was overshadowed by the actions of French coach Daniel Dubroca who grabbed Mr Bishop by the throat after the final whistle and repeatedly called him a cheat.

Dubroca resigned following his outburst, and to the credit of referee Bishop, he made light of the affair saying: "Dubroca, after the game had ended, shook me warmly by the throat."

After five years and 42 appearances for *Les Bleus*, that Rugby World Cup quarter-final was Ondarts' final match in a French jersey.

The following year, his club Biarritz reached the French Championship final at Parc des Princes where they lost 12-19 to Toulon. It was Serge Blanco's last ever rugby match. In 1993 after 17 seasons with the club, Pascal Ondarts hung up his boots for the final time.

The great England and Lions prop Jason Leonard has nothing but admiration and respect for Ondarts.

"Pascal was the most bruising prop I ever played against. Whenever we played France, I knew it would be a bloody battle with bodies strewn everywhere and massive brawls. Ondarts was physically the toughest tighthead I ever faced."

When asked about his toughest opponent, the big Basque without hesitation says Iain Milne of Scotland known as "The Bear".

"He was a huge boy," says Ondarts.

"Another tough customer was Jean-Pierre Garuet, my great friend and fellow French prop. We speak nearly every day."

Incidentally, Garuet was sent off by Welsh referee Clive Norling for gouging in the 1984 Five Nations when France faced Ireland in Paris.

Ondarts could never be described as a try-scoring machine but in the old days props knew their place and very rarely got on the scoresheet.

However, on 11th November 1987 when France faced Romania at Stade Armandie in Agen, a match that *Les Bleus* won by 49-3, Pascal Ondarts scored one of France's seven tries that day along with Marc Andrieu (2) Patrice Lagisquet (2) Philippe Bérot and a penalty try.

It was Pascal's one and only score for the French national team.

France coach Jacques Fouroux's obsession with size meant that Ondarts reached the age of 30 before getting his first cap.

Robert Paparemborde and Pierre Dospital were favoured among other similarly large specimens so he spent what must have seemed like a lifetime playing for France B before getting the call.

Pascal was old school in his post-match regime; there was no warm-down, and hydration took an interesting form. No isotonic drinks for the big Basque, he would start his recovery with Pastis (45% proof). It is indeed the most delightful refreshment on a scorching hot day when served with a pitcher or carafe of ice-cold water. The unique flavour comes from the green anise, a Mediterranean herb, and is enjoyed as much in the dockside bars of Marseilles as in the cafés of the ancient cobbled streets in southern France.

The modern game leaves Pascal with very little to get enthused about.

"I cannot relate to this rugby" he says. "I have reached an age where I only do what interests me. Show me a match lately that enchanted you, that made you vibrate. Personally, I cannot think of one.

"There is no atmosphere in rugby stadiums these days. People come for business and know nothing about the game. It is no longer supporters that go to the match it is customers."

When it comes to customers there is no doubt that Pascal Ondarts is one of the tough variety. His rugby, Pastis and Basque folk singing ensured his selection in my team, plus I didn't want to be the one to have to explain to him why he hadn't been selected.

I'll leave the final words of this chapter to Pascal himself.

"I don't like to look back. The most important day is tomorrow. If I've done something stupid in the past, I'm not interested. What interests me is what I'm going to do in the future. That's my motivation."

Chapter 2

Guilhem Guirado
"How can you govern a country that has 246 varieties of cheese?"
Charles de Gaulle

It is midnight in Saint-Denis, and Guilhem Guirado the France captain is still doing the media rounds. He is muddied, bruised and exhausted after the opening game of the 2019 Guinness Six Nations Championship.

Nine o'clock kick-offs may be good news for the home supporters who can indulge in a leisurely dinner pre-match but for players it is the final knockings of a very long day.

As Friday night nudges into Saturday morning, Guilhem can finally grab a shower. After the endless rounds of media commitments, it is time to start the long process of unwinding. Many more hours will pass before he can finally get the kind of sleep a warrior deserves, although sleep may be in short supply after the extraordinary events that have unfolded on the field of play.

The dark streets of Saint-Denis are illuminated by neon hotel signs, and the dimly-lit bars are nearly empty as the last train takes supporters back to Gare du Nord and central Paris.

An uneasy quiet descends on the Stade de France, the moonlight reflecting in the icy puddles as the shutters on the food outlets come echoing to a close in the Parisian night with the final Espresso dispensed.

On a bitterly cold night, the warm red shirts of Wales created a comeback that would have defied Lazarus as they turned around a 0-16 deficit at half-time, to score three second-half tries and earn a 24-19 victory.

10

It was Wales' biggest ever half-time turnaround in a Five or Six Nations match, and the haunted look and sheer desolation on the French faces at full time was painful to see.

Even with Jefferson Poirot in the front row it is difficult to fathom the mystery of how France let such a big lead slip. What might Poirot the detective have said? "There is nothing more amazing than the extraordinary sanity of the insane! Unless it is the extraordinary eccentricity of the sane!"

Selecting the hooker position for this French Hard Men XV was one of the decisions I struggled with the most.

Firstly, by definition, you don't get a hooker who isn't hard; when you are dangling in a scrum between two brutes with your arms trapped and head-to-head with the opposition, witty repartee is not going to help you very much.

Secondly, France has had such an embarras de richesses of 'talloneurs' – Paco, Dubroca, Szarzewski and Ibanez to name but a few.

I'm sure many will question my choice of Guilhem Guirado as hooker. The numéro deux shirt has been worn by so many wonderful hard men that I really was spoilt for choice. But hardness comes in many different forms and Guilhem Guirado had a mental and physical hardness that very few could match.

He virtually carried the national team at one of the most disappointing periods in its history, but as hooker and captain, Guilhem never let his personal standards or his level of performance drop for one second which is more than can be said for some of his colleagues in the blue jersey.

Guirado was like a one-man battering ram, running himself into the ground, not only doing all the donkey work expected of a hooker but also becoming a major try scorer.

In the 2018 autumn internationals, he scored in all three matches of the series against South Africa, Argentina and Fiji, and ended up as France's top try scorer of the campaign with four.

In total he scored eight tries for his country, four of which came during the fourteen-day period of those 2018 autumn matches.

A Twitter debate perfectly summed up Guilhem's situation. The question was asked: "Which player from another Six Nations team would you select for your own country?"

The overwhelming majority of people voted for Guirado. One user replied: "I would pick Guilhem Guirado just so that he doesn't have to suffer through playing for France anymore!"

Guilhem was a warrior; he put his body on the line time and time again and he never flinched. At the end of every international, the television cameras would pan in on him in painful close-up as he stared wide eyed with despair. Sometimes you got the impression, rightly or wrongly, that he was the only one that cared.

When France lost to Ireland 13-15 at Stade de France in February 2018, Guirado made 31 tackles, a Six Nations record that he jointly holds with Luke Charteris of Wales.

His durability was incredible. For someone who was always the first to put his body on the line, he had very few absences with injury. When Guilhem went down in a match he would invariably bounce back up and if he stayed down then you knew it was something serious.

Arles-sur-Tech is a tiny village, set in a scenic forested valley in the eastern foothills of the Pyrenees, a place where Catalan and French are spoken.

It is less than one hour's drive from the Spanish border, a journey that has a major relevance to one of its inhabitants, Guilhem Guirado.

In stature and appearance, he is exactly how you would imagine a French hooker to look. At 5ft 11ins and 15 stone 8lbs, he is as tough and solid as the local Pyrenean boulders on the field but has the calm, whispering qualities of the meandering Tech river off it.

He is a private man who puts his love of his family above all else. His grandparents were among the half a million Spanish citizens who fled the violence of the Spanish Civil War and crossed the Pyrenees with the sole aim of finding safety and refuge in France. The exodus was the biggest single influx of refugees ever known in France and was named "La Retirada", the Spanish for retreat.

Guilhem's parents were born in Granada. They were both five-year-olds when they arrived in France following that arduous journey with almost nothing to their name.

He says: "Until I was 15 all I knew was this village where my grandparents had arrived, my favourite memories are from here. I loved being that age; it is here everything really started for me and I found a passion for rugby."

Guilhem is a man who knows where he is and more importantly where he has come from.

I first met him at the RBS Six Nations launch in 2016 after he had just been announced as the new France captain. He stood out as a man at peace with himself, taking everything in his stride in a calm and measured manner.

The lovely thing about Guilhem is that the moment he sees you he immediately shows you the latest photos of his children on his mobile phone. We have been through quite a few Six Nations launches and mixed zones together and he is always the same, win or lose.

"To know where you want to go, you need to know about where you came from, and the determination that went before" he says philosophically. When you delve into his family history you get a sense of where that inner strength has come from.

13

"What I like about rugby is the direct confrontation with an opponent, a physical contest and collisions, tackles."

But when he gets home, he puts his bag down and rugby is done and dusted.

"The most important thing for me is my family and the people who are around me, whether they be my parents, grandparents, wife son or daughter."

"It's my stability, it's something that allows me to put things into perspective and to be able to relax and see life in a different way. I'm not only thinking about rugby and that allows me to perform well on the field."

The French region of Pyréneés-Orientales was ceded to France by Spain in the seventeenth century.

This beautiful place, nestled between the Pyrenees mountains and the Mediterranean Sea, is part of Northern Catalonia, also known as French Catalonia.

Perpignan accounts for over a quarter of the population of Northern Catalonia and is the heartbeat of Catalan culture and gastronomy. You will certainly find more red and yellow horizontally striped flags here than Tricolores.

While Catalonia is the richest part of Spain, French Catalonia is one of the poorest regions of France.

Guirado is a proud Catalan and to play for USAP was his boyhood dream.

To play for Union Sportive des Arlequins Perpignanais to give them their full title is a local aspiration akin to the boys on the Copacabana wanting to play for Brazil. For Guilhem it was no different.

"My first game for Perpignan was on 8th August 2006 in a local derby against Narbonne. I remember we played three matches in nine days. I arrived at the club aged 14. I never imagined playing for the first team. By just playing for the juniors, I felt I had reached my pinnacle."

He broke his leg at the age of 15, an injury which should have been resolved in a few months but in this instance Guilhem was out of action for over a year.

14

"I watched my first Perpignan match in May 1998 and my whole life has flowed from it. I always wanted to outdo myself for the club for which I had such a wonderful attachment" says Guirado.

His final match for USAP ended in a heartbreaking defeat to Clermont, a result that confirmed their relegation to the second division, the ProD2.

"I used that awful feeling to motivate me throughout my career" he says. But there were also some wonderful moments at a club where you sense Guilhem's Catalan heart still beats strongly.

"Two of my greatest rugby moments were the 2019 Top 14 Final win with USAP and the European Cup quarter final against Toulon which was played at Montjuïc in Barcelona. It was a wonderful Catalan occasion played in front of a packed crowd in the Olympic Stadium and a win for us 29-26."

After nine years, 202 matches and 20 tries at Perpignan, he moved 381 kilometers along the coast to Toulon and became part of the star-studded team that won the European Cup at Twickenham on 2nd May 2015 when they beat Clermont 24-18.

Leigh Halfpenny, Juan Martín Hernández, Drew Mitchell, Juan Smith and Bakkies Botha all played for Toulon that day.

Guirado's playing career has included Perpignan, Toulon and Montpellier along with an international career that ended in the land of the rising scrum on 20th October 2019 when France were defeated in the Rugby World Cup quarter final by Wales.

"My first memory is the first time I played rugby; it was with all my friends in Arles-sur-Tech and the most beautiful thing is we all got to know each other on the rugby field and today we are still sharing our lives and great moments together."

15

"I have been lucky to be able to play for my club that made me dream when I was a kid, the Perpignan team USAP, and finally to be able to play with France a few years later and then to play with Toulon and Montpellier with the best players in the oval world."

He won his first international cap for France on 9th March 2008, replacing Dimitri Szarzewski and coming off the bench against Italy at the Stade de France in a 25-13 victory. "I remember my first cap, a special taste, I remember it like it was yesterday."

"It was a great pride, a huge honour for all that it means for me and for France."

Guilhem never took for granted the responsibility and honour of putting on the French jersey.

"I think it's always an honour to play for and represent France, everything goes more quickly, and it is a bit stressful because of the fear of not being up to the mark. You want your family to be proud of you."

"I like to know what has happened in the past and immerse myself in it because I also have to represent all the former players. There have been some huge players and great hookers who have gone before me."

"For me this shirt really represents the welcome given to the Spanish exiles. I am French. I grew up in France; it is a country that was ready to give a welcome to my grandparents so of course I think of them."

Guirado had to battle for a starting place in the French team with William Servat and Szarzewski, two very talented hookers. But he eventually got his first start in the 2010 November international against Fiji.

Jacques Brunel, who had worked with Guilhem at Perpignan, became French coach after the 2015 Rugby World Cup, and he named Guirado as his captain for the 2016 Six Nations. His debut as skipper came against Italy at Stade de France, a match that took on an important significance after Paris had suffered several terrorist atrocities during the latter part of 2015.

There was a nervous eerie build-up to the game, and to see so many armed police and military personnel at a rugby match made for an unusual experience. But on a mild sunny day in the French capital, the national anthem was sung with even more emotion than usual and you could feel the crowd relax as the match progressed.

The whole occasion, and a win for *Les Bleus*, brought a much-needed smile to a city that had suffered so much.

France won 23-21 through tries by Vakatawa, Chouly and Bonneval although the joy was very nearly curtailed at the very end of the match when a Sergio Parisse drop goal attempt drifted wide.

"In my first match as captain everything went very fast" he says. "Meeting new staff and new players meant an awful lot of pressure."

Guirado went on to captain France on 33 occasions, winning 12, losing 20 and drawing one.

On captaincy, he says: "I don't have a specific style; it is mainly a feeling, a lot of conversations and a lot of questioning and the captain is nothing without the players around him."

Following France's defeat to England at Twickenham in 2019, the coaching staff wanted to relieve Guirado of his duties and promote Bordeaux prop, Jefferson Poirot to the captain's role.

Poirot refused and the players backed Guilhem by taking a stand and making their feelings clear to the management that they wanted the Toulon hooker to continue as skipper.

France got back to winning ways in their next game against Scotland at a sun-drenched Stade de France and one incident in that game exemplified Guirado's unfussy, nononsense tough-as-teak approach. As Scotland's Grant Gilchrist pulled a pass back to Peter Horne, he was lined up and demolished in a thunderous tackle by the French skipper. Guirado just got up off the floor with no fuss and launched himself into another big hit.

Not much was made of the initial tackle until it was shown on the big screen. It was only then that the big crowd realized what a massive hit it had been. As they did so, the whole crowd gave out a collective gasp. It was a microcosm of Guilhem's career. No fist pumps, no showboating just getting on with the job and leading by example.

Guilhem's seventy-fourth and final match for France took place on 28th October 2018 at the Bank Dome in Ōita at the quarter final stage of the 2019 Rugby World Cup.

In an enthralling match during which France played superbly, *Les Bleus* scored three tries through Vahaamahina, Ollivon and Vakatawa and led 19-10 at the break.

In the 48th minute, Vahaamahina was red-carded for elbowing Aaron Wainwright in the head, a foolish act that turned out to be a game-changing moment, and with just 14 men France could only stem the red tide for so long before they eventually succumbed to a last- minute try that gave Wales victory by a single point, 20-19.

After holding the national team together through the dark times, Guirado called it a day, safe in the knowledge that France had rediscovered their rugby mojo.

A new and exciting youthful group of players were at the start of something special, and in the match against Wales they showed that the Gallic phoenix had risen from the ashes. It was time for Captain Courageous to call it a day.

The weeks following the Wales defeat were difficult for him. His moving speech in the changing room after that game was plastered all over social media and showed a side to Guirado that had remained private, a persona reserved for the inner sanctum of the French squad.

The public liked what they saw as he spoke with emotion and eloquence. It emphasized his credentials as a leader, as he put aside his own emotions after his final international to inspire those who would carry the baton through to the next Rugby World Cup. This was just typical of the man.

Guirado signed for Montpellier prior to the 2019 Rugby World Cup, having spent five years at Toulon where he played 110 matches and scored 11 tries. He was a huge favourite with the loyal fans at the Stade Mayol.

"I think I need the sea to live" he says.

"To succeed you need good living conditions. Montpellier want to establish themselves at the top and win titles. The move was a very important decision that required a lot of thought."

In December 2019 he made his Montpellier debut against, of all teams, Toulon, at the Stade Mayol. The match ended in a 19-19 draw. Guirado didn't finish the match after tearing his right bicep off the bone.

However, the following season ended on a much happier note as Guilhem lifted the European Challenge Cup trophy at Twickenham on 21st May 2021 as Montpellier defeated Leicester in a pulsating final.

He retired from the game at the end of the 2021-22 season and it will be interesting to see what the future holds for Guilhem, a thoroughly decent man who gave everything for club and country.

Whatever happens, you sense that Guilhem will take it all in his stride. His mother says: "He must never forget where he is from, it is his strength." And as we all know, mothers are usually right.

Chapter 3

Gérard Cholley
"Terror is only justice: prompt severe and inflexible. It is then an emanation of virtue."
Maximilien Robespierre

Paratrooper, boxer, potato farmer and chauffeur to high-ranking French officials, whoever gets the film rights to *The Gérard Cholley Story* will do well at the box office. The top of the props, regarded by the majority of his opponents as the most frightening and most difficult to play against, has had a career (and a life) that could fill a thousand pages and plenty of screen time.

The man from Fontaine-lès-Luxeuil, a small commune in the Haute-Saône department, was voted the most frightening Frenchman of all time by *The Sunday Times* newspaper in 2006, an accolade that the big man took as a compliment rather than an insult. "No, it's a compliment for sure. In some matches I used to start on the loosehead and then move across to the other side if our tighthead was having a problem. I would sort out the problem."

Gérard had his own style of problem-solving which he administered with glee. It nearly always resulted in pain for the individual perceived to be the root of the problem.

When you look at some of the other candidates for the top spot in the poll, many of whom are mentioned in this book, it shows just how menacing the 6ft 4in prop actually was. He was one of the first names on my team sheet just for the sheer terror he would create when the opposition discovered his name in the match programme.

One of the essentials of being a true rugby hard man is to be in the possession of a decent nickname.

Whatever your nationality, or position, you cannot be seriously considered as a candidate for the Hall of Pain unless you possess this must-have accoutrement.

Samoa's Brian Lima known as "The Chiropractor" due to way he rearranges bones in the tackle and Brian Moore of England ("Pitbull") have nicknames that fit the bill perfectly, as does Springbok prop Tendai Mtawarira who is known as "The Beast."

Some players sadly end up with slightly less menacing and fearsome nicknames. Take former French captain and coach Philippe Georges Saint-André for example, who was saddled with "Le Goret" which translates to "Piglet", a title he earned due to his shuffling running style.

As for Cholley, well he was special; he had a journal full of nicknames, the top three being "The Master of Menace", "Le Guv'nor" and the most often used and the one that I will employ for the purposes of this France XV, "Le Patron" or in English "The Boss".

Cholley's scary face bore the ingrained traces of hardness in every line and wrinkle which somehow seemed to mirror his on-field activities. When he smiled it was even more frightening, the resulting look being a cross between Muttley, the cartoon dog from *Wacky Races*, and a hungry serial killer.

Fact and fiction often merge when people talk about Gerard Cholley but the facts are much more incredible than the fictional versions in his case.

The great English and Lions prop Fran Cotton once said that "Cholley was like a huge night club bouncer going to work. You could not take your eyes off him for 80 minutes. He was always up to no good."

But it is often forgotten that Cholley was also a brilliant scrum technician who could switch between loosehead and tighthead.

He boxed in his youth before being called up for national service as an 18-year-old. Those skills earned as a callow youngster were to stand him in good stead when he turned to the oval ball game.

In 1965, in the last month of his military service, he went into a café in Castres. The owner took one look at him and saw what a handy asset he would be to the local rugby team. He told him: "You're a big lad, you should be playing rugby."

Cholley served with the 8th Marine Infantry Parachute Regiment, an elite regiment and part of the 11th Parachute Brigade garrisoned in Castres. These are French airborne units specializing in air combat and assault. All I can say is those parachutes must have been made of sturdy stuff, and one of the very few things that could bring Gerard Cholley to ground both in the literal and abstract sense.

The coveted red beret he donned during his 18-month service is still worn with immense pride at Remembrance occasions by the big man.

Cholley had never played in, or even watched a rugby match, but he went along with the team to watch an away fixture a week later and ended up playing. He knew nothing about rugby, but during the match a fight broke out and as he said later: "I thought: 'Ah! This is the sport for me!'" Within two weeks he was playing for the first XV.

He began his rugby career in the second row before switching to prop. Learning as he went along, he says he was very strong in the back but also very flexible which helped him in his quest to heap misery on opposition props.

The fact that Cholley spent his entire career at Castres is a testament to his loyalty and to the club who looked after him.

Castres Olympique, to give them their full title, were formed in 1898 when several men from Castres Municipal College met in a bar and decided to form a team.

As well as winning five French championships, the most recent in 2018, the club have produced some outstanding international players for *Les Bleus*, including Hard Men XV candidate flanker Alain Carminati, props Benjamin Kayser and Pascal Papé along with one of the most niggly centres of all time, Richard Dourthe, a man who could start a fight in a convent.

Some great overseas players have spent time at the club; All Blacks Gary Whetton, Frank Bunce, Rudi Wulf and Kees Meeuws have all graced Stade Pierre-Fabre.

Cholley made his France debut, along with Jean-Pierre Rives, at Twickenham in 1975. France were victorious by 27 points to 20. They outscored England by four tries to two with Etchenique, Gourdon, Guilbert and Claude Spanghero touching down for the visitors while Duckham and Rossborough scored for England.

Cholley's arrival on the international scene caused a great a deal of amusement among the French squad. He turned up to his first team meeting in a shirt, tie and a three-piece suit with a matching man bag.

It was a winning start for Cholley at Twickenham and the first of 31 caps for the national side.

His fellow prop that day was Armand Vaquerin and if you think Cholley's story is an interesting one then Vaquerin's is bizarre to say the least.

In any other Hard Man XV, Vaquerin would have been a shoo-in but when you are talking about France, and in particular French props, then your brutality cup runneth over.

The highly decorated Vaquerin won ten top 14 titles in the 1970s during his career at Béziers. His life ended tragically one night when he entered Bar Le Cardiff in Béziers to play a game of Russian roulette with a revolver he just happened to have on his person.

In an effort to enlist some playing partners, he pointed the gun at his head and pulled the trigger thinking that the gun was empty. A solitary bullet remained in the chamber. You can guess the rest.

He is still venerated in Béziers where the locals are reluctant to discuss the events of that tragic evening.

A statue outside Bézier's ground, the beautiful Stade de la Méditerranée, has been erected showing Vaquerin lifting the French championship trophy, the Bouclier de Brennus, commemorating him and his ten championship-winning medals.

When France played Wales in the 1970s, the game usually decided the winner of the Five Nations, and more often than not, there was a Grand Slam at stake.

The French front row coming up against their Welsh counterparts, who also happened to be the Pontypool front row, was a recipe for full-scale brutality and with that wonderful trio of Graham Price, Bobby Windsor and Charlie Faulkner come a volume of tales that will live on in rugby history.

While preparing this book I spoke to Graham and Bobby. I caught "Pricey" in the Principality Stadium press room where he relayed the story of the 1976 Grand Slam decider in Cardiff.

"When I first played against Cholley, in 1976, I had been informed that he was a good scrummager, incredibly strong, and that he didn't take any prisoners."

"At the first scrum, he clawed at my face ferociously. My arms were trapped so I sank my teeth into Cholley's thumb. He squealed and complained to the referee, but the ref went over to lecture Bobby [Windsor] and Bobby's startled look of innocence was amazing."

But worse was to come a bit later. Graham continued: "I was trying to set up a ruck and was stuck between Michel Palmié and Jean-François Imbernon. Cholley came from behind and started raking at my eyes. I ended up with a scratched cornea and had to leave the field. I missed the team dinner that night and all the Grand Slam celebrations as I had to go home and lie with my eye closed. There was a fear that I might lose my sight, but thankfully that didn't happen."

Cholley recalls: "The day before the match I had a fever of 39 degrees and I was as sick as a dog, so I pumped myself full of vitamin C. I was so wound up on match day that I punched the ceiling in the Arms Park dressing room and part of it fell down on the shoulder of our second row Jean-Francois Imbernon. We weren't sure whether he would miss the game due to the resulting injury but fortunately after receiving attention he was able to play."

Bobby Windsor described Gerard Cholley himself as "A fearsome bloke with a neck the size of an Aberdeen Angus bull."

The late great commentator Bill McLaren had a wonderful way with words, and the French front rows provided him with so much material, producing such unique quotes as: "They got faces like a bag of chisels" and "He's built like a bicycle shed that fella."

Cholley recalls that 1976 match in Cardiff and says: "Wales dominated rugby at that time, and when we played them that day, we had special plans for J. P. R. Williams. He was a back who liked to get involved with the forwards, but he only did it once that day. We absolutely hammered him. I won't say what we did to him ..." he says what that sinister grin of his.

"We were preparing to go to war, and when you play an international match, you don't need external motivation, it happens naturally."

"The following year (1977) we beat Wales, in Paris and won a Grand Slam but we did not talk of revenge. When you play for France, you have to win every match, for your country, your family, your friends, and for you."

Gerard Cholley gave one of his most notorious performances for France in 1977 when *Les Bleus*, playing in white, faced Scotland at Parc des Princes.

Ian Barnes played against him that day and described him as looking like "Moby Dick in a goldfish bowl."

Cholley punched Donald MacDonald in a line-out, and at least three other Scotsmen during the match, his collection of casualties being obtained in a manner likened to that of a "bus conductor proceeding up the aisle taking fares" according to colourful reports at the time.

MacDonald was stretchered off, and although the referee that day, Welshman Merion Joseph, wagged his finger all game, amazingly not one French player received his marching orders. The Scots were pretty incensed with the punches off the ball, the gouging, the stamping on heads but for the French this was the normal way of things.

Cholley recalls that "French Rugby Federation president, Albert Ferrasse, told me he would be one step ahead of the Scottish president who wanted my guts for garters. He told me he would lecture me, then told me to keep my head down, that way the Scottish official won't be able to say anything more."

Iain Henderson remembers lining up in the tunnel that day in Paris and describing the French as a gang of people who looked like they'd just been released from the Bastille prison.

This was not a one-off incident for "Le Patron" who, when one of the French team was set upon in a tour match in South Africa, managed to knock out three Western Province forwards in retaliation.

Scotland have often been the victims of choice for the French particularly when playing at home.

For a long period in recent years, *Les Bleus* have been a shadow of their former selves both in the fists and flair departments. In fact, the national women's team have been a much harder proposition, as Scotland and Harlequins lock Deborah McCormack can testify. Debs gained her thirtieth cap against the French in Lille in 2019, one of six

26

appearances she made against the French between 2014 and 2020.

"The French forwards in particular were always so physical and appeared to look so much bigger than other opposition packs, particularly Safi N'Diaye and Lénaïg Corson, I just seemed to be constantly tackling a rampaging sea of blue when I was up against them."

To give you some perspective, N'Diaye weighed in at just under 15 stones and was six feet tall.

On 11th November 1997, prop (and amateur wrestler) Gary Knight made his All Black debut against France in Toulouse. Cholley eye-gouged him and tore his eyelid. This was the same year that the Frenchman punched the Lansdowne Road dressing room ceiling so hard that he put his fist right through. As a result, his hand swelled to the size of a melon, but he still played as France beat Ireland 15-6.

Cholley bowed out of international rugby at Parc des Princes, his personal Madison Square Garden, on 17th March 1979 in front of 45,000 fans. This was two years after his punch fest and once again Scotland were the visitors.

As in his debut four years earlier, Cholley finished on the winning side with France narrowly defeating a talented Scottish outfit 21-17.

Scotland had held France 10-10 at half-time with their classy back line of Andy Irvine, Keith Robertson, Jim Renwick, Ian McGeechan and Bruce Hay plus the half-back pairing of John Rutherford and Bill McLaren's son-in-law Alan Lawson to the fore.

The teams scored three tries apiece: Dickson, Irvine and Robertson for Scotland. And for France, number eight Yves Malquier scored twice on his debut along with one try from Christian Bélascain.

In August 1997, Cholley had the honour to be selected for a World XV team to face South Africa in a special match to commemorate the opening of the Loftus Versfeld Stadium in Pretoria.

A team captained by legendary Irishman Willie John McBride and coached by Syd Millar were defeated by the Boks 45-24. It was a stellar side that included J. P. R. Williams, Gerald Davies, Gareth Edwards, Ian Kirkpatrick, Hugo Porta and Cholley's compatriot Jean-Pierre Rives.

Try-scoring was not a part of Cholley's remit, but he did score three for France, his first against Ireland at Parc des Princes on 7th February 1976, the opening try of the match in a 26-3 win for the men in blue. Eight months later he went on a bit of a scoring spree with two tries in seven days on 24th and 30th October. The venues were Bordeaux and Paris respectively and the opponents Australia.

Eight years after his international retirement, Castres honoured the big prop with a testimonial match in 1987. It was attended by many of the Welsh players who had been on the receiving end of Cholley's enforcement practices, and to prove his heart was as big as his right hook, he donated all the money raised to a mental health charity.

The scrum was Cholley's theatre of war. "In the scrum, I feared no one" he says. "I may have been a bad guy on the field but afterwards I always drank an apéritif with the opposition."

"I was great friends with Armand Vaquerin, the Béziers and France prop. We smashed each other senseless when we played against each other but at the final whistle we would fall into each other's arms."

"Graham Price of Wales was a great prop but that did not prevent him retreating when he was put under pressure. We had some battles, the two of us."

The big man's greatest regret is that he didn't start playing earlier; he was aged 30 when he won his first cap.

"I would have loved to play in the modern era. I would have really enjoyed myself; I would have done bodybuilding all week, I was a training freak, I loved it but at Castres we only trained twice a week."

"But I would be bored in the scrums. These days opponents knock you down and you can't even punch them. And the general fights no longer exist; now they all do the tango!"

As you might imagine, Gerard Cholley feels no need to apologize for the way he played the game and sums up his philosophy in a single sentence that smacks of Oscar Wilde. "In life what matters is not whether you're talked about in nice way or a bad way but just that you are talked about."

Chapter 4

Walter Spanghero

"They have a very low rate for attempted murder and a high rate for successfully concluded murder. It seems that when a French person sets out to kill someone, they make a good job of it."

Nick Yapp

Fleeing Mussolini and fascism in Italy proved to be a major factor in the production of one of the true legends of French rugby, Walter Spanghero.

The lock, or second row, is one of the positions France have filled over the years with some true rugby greats. Alongside the front row, it has proved to be the natural habitat of the hard man.

Tucked between the props and the back row, it offers the perfect concealment to launch attacks on the opposition pack. These attacks can take the form of serious scrummaging technique or indeed some well-timed skullduggery.

The additional territory of the middle of the line-out, occupied by these beasts, is another location where there is ample opportunity to wreak havoc. An elbow here, a boot there, a stamp on the opposite jumper's foot; there is a host of weaponry that can be deployed.

There were many candidates for the lock positions in my XV, and I pondered long and hard over many a night, with only a glass of Saint-Émilion for comfort. This selection business is not as easy as I thought.

One of the beasts of Béziers, Michel Palmié, capped at lock 23 times between 1971 and 1978, received a lifetime ban for partially blinding Armand Clerc of Racing Club following a punch-up. Palmié had punched his way across the country, covering all points of the compass and finally went one step too far. Bizarrely, Palmié later went on to become an official in the French Rugby Federation.

Fellow second row, Olivier Merle, won 45 caps at lock for France between 1993 and 1997. Known as "Le Massif Central" he headbutted Wales and Llanelli prop Ricky Evans in Paris, causing a ruck to collapse and resulting in a broken ankle for the Welshman.

Merle was successfully sued, and Evans received damages for loss of earnings as a result of the incident. Merle never played again for France.

Jean-François Imbernon and Jean Condom, who never practiced safe rugby, were another two hard men who patrolled the French line-out in the Seventies.

Alain Estève, another Béziers bearded bruiser, also stood out in that decade. Former Welsh hooker Bobby Windsor recalls one encounter when Wales faced France at Parc des Princes in Paris.

"I was getting slaughtered in the scrums, Estève was throwing the punches through, and I couldn't do anything about it because my arms were around my two props," he recalls.

"So, I said to Charlie [Faulkner]: 'We've got to do something about this or I'm dead meat. Next time he goes down we've got to give him a right booting to shut him up.'"

Sure enough, down went Estève again and the pair of them lashed into him, certain that would be the end of him as a threat. But far from it. "I couldn't believe it when he got up and he gave me a big wink and said: 'Bob-eee, next time I get you!'"

"So, I turned to Charlie and said: 'Did you hear that? I'm in for it this time. What are we gonna do now?' Faulkner replied quick-as-a-flash: 'Tell him he's wanted on the telephone.'"

More recently, one of the truly great players Fabien Pelous, the most capped Frenchman of all time, graced the

French second row for 12 years earning the man from Toulouse 118 caps. He was also captain on 42 occasions.

But for me, Walter Spanghero just had to be in the team. He was as hard as nails with thuggery kept to the minimum although 'minimum' in the French club matches of his era amounted to a fair old bit. What he did have was power, pace and an engine that Rolls Royce would have been proud of.

The late great New Zealand legend Colin "Pine Tree" Meads told a tale about when France played New Zealand in Paris in 1967.

"I was kicked in the back of the head and had to leave the field. I returned stitched up, covered in bandages and sticking plaster and not happy. I had been warned that Benoît Dauga was a bit of thug, so later in the game I punched him on the nose. At the post-match function, he came up to me and pointed at his nose which was now spread across his face and said: 'Why you do this?' I replied: 'You know why, you dirty bastard!' He says: 'Non, non – it wasn't me. It was Spanghero!'"

Located some 786 kilometers south of Paris, Narbonne is a city of just over 50,000 people. It was an important Roman seaport but silting of the river Aude for centuries has meant that it is now situated 15 kilometers inland. It is linked to the nearby Canal du Midi and the Aude by the Canal de la Robine that flows through the centre of town.

It is also the birthplace of the legendary French crooner Charles Trenet, famous for his recordings between the 1930s and 1950s, his most popular songs being "La Mer" and "Boum!" The latter could quite appropriately be used as Walter Spanghero's theme tune.

If you ask anyone in Narbonne what the town is most famous for, you will probably be told, "Walter Spanghero."

In these days of being called a legend just for getting a cup of coffee for someone, Walter truly was a legend, a

French rugby legend as well as one of the country's greatest players of all time.

A big family in every sense of the word, the Spanghero brothers make *The Sopranos* look like *Swiss Family Robinson.* The Four Horsemen of the Apocalypse would have a job on their hands with Walter and his five brothers Laurent, Jean-Marie, Claude, Guy and Gilbert, not forgetting his two sisters Annie and Maryse. There were often 18 family members at the meal table, and when you look at the size of the brothers, it's quite evident that meat portions were not a soupçon or amuse-bouche.

All six brothers played rugby for Narbonne when it was a major force in French club rugby.

The father, Ferruccio Dante Spanghero, fled his hometown of Friuli and escaped Italy during the rise of fascism and a national onset of poverty. He was a stone mason in his native land before settling in the village of Bram near Castelnaudary where he became a farmer.

I'm not sure what they put in the water in Friuli, but Spanghero senior and his wife Romea reared some pretty hefty citizens.

Walter admitted: "I do feel a little bit Italian, and I always follow the results of Italian sports. As a teenager, we listened on the family radio to follow the exploits of Bartali [cyclist] or mountaineer Walter Bonatti or the heavyweight Primo Carnera but I have worn the French jersey with great pride and joy."

Spanghero says: "Our parental background, as immigrants from Friuli, in Italy's Dolomite Mountains, has made us lovers of the land."

"My brothers and I were brought up to make sure a job was well done. At 12 or 13 years old, I had to milk the cows at 5 a.m. before going to school and do the same in the evening when I came home.

"I was the most restless of all my brothers. I couldn't stay still and yearned for large open spaces. I left school at

14 because it was impossible for me to sit for any prolonged period behind a desk.

"My father told me: 'If you can't study, then you'll work for me on the farm. There is plenty of work in the fields.' But this departure from school remains a bad memory because I have sometimes missed studies in my professional life."

The Spanghero brothers discovered that rugby was like their life on the land. "Rugby was for us a wonderful discovery, a catalyst and a great learning experience. Apart from the four walls of the farm and the expanse of the fields, we knew little about life and were not very streetwise.

"Sport puts you in the spotlight. Even when I first started out with Bram, I suddenly found myself a village celebrity.

"As a family we are people who never wanted to disappoint, treasuring a principle that from the moment you are trusted, you must not betray that trust. We were given this confidence in the clubs, in Bram, in the Racing Club de Narbonne then in the French team. This is why we have always needed to prove, to explode, to have fun and in return to give pleasure. In a word, we had the means, with rugby, to live even more strongly."

Walter continues: "In both cases, we are talking about a work of valour, strength, constancy, and a desire for self-denial. As in the game of rugby, working the land was also based on a collective spirit. We went to the fields with four or five, we harvested even more. If someone among us fell behind, the others helped him so that we could continue together and arrive together at the end of the vine. So many qualities that we had to develop every Sunday on the stadiums. We practised, so to speak, natural training by going back and forth in the fields, by carrying with bare hands straw bales or sacks of wheat. We were physically ready.

"Today, as this physical engagement in agricultural work is no longer in effect, one sits on the tractor and the tractor pulls the load. So, it is necessary to compensate by weight training, sprinting and modern forms of training.

"To take an example from my own career, I experienced a big slump during the 1969-1970 season. I had just left the farm to become a city man. I was not physically strong enough anymore. I tried to compensate with a lot of bodybuilding. I may have become the most beautiful on the beach with strong pectoral muscles and strong muscular thighs but on the pitch, I was not going any further. A terrible year. I even thought of stopping rugby. I stopped weight-training and replaced it with laps of the stadium, fractional sprints and mounds. The useless muscle mass disappeared. I thus found all my juice."

The brothers set up a meat business, but Walter's love of animals meant he did not want to be involved so he concentrated on the automobile arm of the family portfolio, managing Sud Ouest Autos in Toulouse which is now run by his son Xavier.

I can only imagine that the family ate most of the stock of their meat business, particularly Walter and Claude, who both went on to play for France.

As Bill McLaren once said of the Quinnell brothers, Scott and Craig: "They're a couple of well-nourished individuals." The same could be said about the Spanghero boys.

Rugby success began in the orange shirt of Narbonne, but business success originated some 60 kilometres west in the town of Castelnaudary.

The company Maison Spanghero, founded by brothers Claude and Laurent, was a €100m- a-year food business that supplied supermarkets with cassoulet, the signature dish of the south-west. It's a slow cooked casserole containing meat – typically pork sausage, goose, duck and haricot beans. It is named after the deep round earthenware pot with slanting sides that the original recipe was cooked in.

The cassoulet has almost religious status in Languedoc. The organization the Grand Brotherhood of the Cassoulet of Castelnaudary arrange annual competitions and fairs featuring their revered produce.

Walter Spanghero made his debut for France against South Africa in 1964 as a 20-year-old. There were not many more daunting teams to play against at that time than the Boks, and to make your international debut against them on their patch, at such a tender age, was some challenge.

France had been searching for a heavy, fast, ball-carrying forward for some time and Walter fitted the bill perfectly. He added mobility and pace to a French team that emerged victorious 8-6.

Spanghero had been a late choice for the tour when Toulouse Number 8 Jean Fabre dropped out. He joined Benoît Dauga in the second row and their partnership became a stable fixture leading up to France's first ever Grand Slam in 1968.

"A beautiful runner and ball player, with the biggest hands I've ever seen, who epitomized all that was best in French forward play" was how the late great Mervyn Davies described Spanghero.

On his debut, France won the battle up-front, confining the Boks to their own half for long periods. *Les Bleus* took control with a superb try by wing Christian Darrouy who charged 50 metres up the touchline to score just before half-time. The Boks had a last-minute penalty chance to win the match, but the kick failed, leaving France winners by 8-6.

Like Colin Meads, Spanghero could play either lock or Number 8 although unlike the New Zealander he alternated between the two positions for his whole career, winning 23 caps in each position.

He also won five caps on the flank, most memorably in Cardiff in 1968, when a late injury to Jean Salut led to a wholesale reshuffle of the French pack which proved entirely successful as they completed their first ever Grand Slam.

Salut had an interesting time the following year, when replacements were allowed for the first time in the Five Nations Championship.

The blond flanker of Russian heritage was selected for France's opening match of the 1969 tournament against Scotland in Paris.

Misfortune struck when he twisted his ankle while leaving the dressing room for the warm- up and was given a pain killing injection. Then as he ran out with the team prior to kick-off, he turned his ankle running up the steps to the pitch at Stade Colombes and fell heavily. This resulted in prop Jean Iracabal taking his place and saw Spanghero move to flanker to fill the position vacated by the unfortunate Salut.

The match was won by Scotland 6-3 thanks to a late try by Jim Telfer of British Lions coaching fame.

Scotland did not taste victory in Paris for a further 26 years.

France arrived at Cardiff Arms Park on 23rd March 1968 chasing their first ever Grand Slam.

They had beaten Scotland at Murrayfield on a wintry January day by 8 points to 6.

A fortnight later, France entertained Ireland in Paris and won convincingly 16-6, after defeating England 14-9 in a close encounter at Colombes (England had led 6-3 at half-time) on 24th February.

The pitch was very wet and heavy, but the wind helped to improve conditions as the match wore on.

Wales started brightly with right wing Keri Jones scoring a try for Wales before Guy Camberabero dropped a goal for the visitors.

Rees kicked a penalty for Wales to give them a 9-3 half-time lead.

The Welsh pack dominated proceedings and things looked ominous for France. However, in the second half, with Wales playing into the wind, fly-half Barry John kicked inaccurately and France took the lead when Lilian Camberabero, brother of Guy, attempted a drop goal which struck a Welsh player and dropped under the posts so allowing French captain, flanker Christian Carrère, to touch down for a try. Guy Camberabero converted to make the score Wales 9 France 8.

With the match in the balance, France were awarded a scrum near the Wales try line. Carrère gathered and passed to scrum-half Lilian Camberabero on the blind side who dived for the line to make a crucial score. The conversion attempt failed but France now led 11-9.

Doug Rees missed a penalty for Wales, right in front of the posts, before hooker Jeff Young tackled Élie Cester without the ball so allowing Guy Camberabero to land a penalty and make it 14-9 to France which was the final score.

Spanghero recalls: "The Camberabero brothers from La Voulte were carried off the field by the rest of us shoulder-high as the pair had scored 11 of France's 14 points. It was a day I will never forget."

Spanghero's quality was testified to by one the greatest players in his two main positions. Colin Meads remembered the King Country vs France match in 1968. "He gave me a pasting in the line-outs that day or at least he made it difficult." More generally, Meads' summation was that the Frenchman was "a fair player who went for the ball all the time, spring-heeled on the jump and as tough as teak."

Meads, an All Blacks legend, went on to describe Spanghero as: "The most docile delightful man off the field, and in a match hard but mostly scrupulously fair."

Spanghero shone on his second tour to South Africa in 1967 and was to earn the nickname "Iron Man" from the Springbok supporters.

He was made French captain in 1969 with the national team in disarray after 10 consecutive defeats. A big supporter of Spanghero's elevation to captain was the French president, Georges Pompidou.

The ten-match losing run ended with an 11-11 draw against Wales, a game best remembered for Phil Bennett's debut as the first ever Welsh replacement.

But Walter fell out of favour with the French selectors and was dropped. Coach Guy Basquet decided that he had to choose between Spanghero and Dauga and the latter got the nod.

Spanghero complained that Basquet had "made a laughingstock of him." He was however recalled as captain in 1972, inspiring France to a 37-12 victory over England.

The press lavished praise on Spanghero when France beat the All Blacks 13-6 in Paris in 1973; they claimed he was the man of the match with his "fantastic mobility, his line-out dominance and his freedom fighter heart." Then, after leading France to an unusual five-way tie in the Five Nations Championship in 1973, he announced his international retirement.

The one serious gap in his list of honours was a national club championship; his club Narbonne were champions way back in 1936 and did nothing spectacular until 1964 when they reached the semi-finals.

After reaching further semi-finals in 1968 and 1972, they eventually made it to the final in 1974 and faced their local rivals from just down the road, Béziers, who were the dominant team of the Seventies in France.

A Narbonne side led by Walter, and including not only Claude but yet another brother, Jean-Marie, were within seconds of victory when the Béziers outside-half, Henri Cabrol, landed a drop goal to snatch the title.

There was a further semi-final loss in 1975 to Agen by 22-6. By the time Narbonne finally claimed the venerable shield under brother Claude's leadership in 1979, Walter had moved on for a career swan song with Toulouse where he spent two seasons playing in the back row alongside Jean-Pierre Rives and Jean-Claude Skrela. That was one heck of a back row!

After that, Walter became a municipal councilor of the city of Toulouse in 2001 before resigning to run a pound shop company.

Walter was very much one of rugby's old school and once said: "A match that doesn't hurt you is a match wasted." On being told that training at altitude helped increase your red blood cell count, he said that the best way to up the count was to drink a bottle of red. And if there was a drugs test: "Drink a bottle of white to restore the balance."

Since he underwent a series of eye operations a few years ago, he admits things are slowing him down.

When asked what his golf handicap is, he replies: "My hands – they are so big I can't pick the ball out of the holes!"

Part of the family business empire incorporated the renowned Table de Spanghero food label that was implicated in the 2013 horse meat scandal.

In 2009 the brothers sold their majority holding of the company to French food giant Lur Berri, a condition of the sale being that the company retained the Spanghero name.

It was no longer under Spanghero control, but Walter spoke of his embarrassment and the feeling that he was being pointed at and talked about in the street. He almost certainly was, but it is a fair bet that most of the pointing and talking was in respect of his stature as one of France's great rugby players.

Walter Spanghero played 51 times for France scoring four tries and played alongside brother Claude on seven occasions. The pair had a stormy off-field relationship, but on the pitch they were united. Claude took over from Walter at number eight in the national side when the elder Spanghero retired.

There is no doubt that his work on the farm gave him a strength and physique that would have been difficult to replicate in a gym and it also provided him with a long career uninterrupted by injury.

To watch the big man play was like witnessing one of the wild white horses of the Camargue galloping through the salt marshes, his mane held back with a white headband as he strode majestically across his fields of dreams. He often carried the ball one-handed, off-loading like a Gallic Fijian. Italy's loss was very definitely France's gain.

Chapter 5

Sebastién Chabal
"The French Riviera, a sunny place for shady people."
Somerset Maugham

"The bulging thighs, the throbbing biceps, the just-back-from-the-hunt grooming. They call him the Caveman; from some angles he looks feral. I've never heard him speak but from one look you can tell that this Fred Flintstone would see that his Wilma never went without."

These words that colourfully describe Sebastién Chabal's qualities were written by one of his many fans.

His career from caveman to chambermaid, and the multi-faceted roles of rugby player, celebrity and sex symbol, have taken his fame and popularity well beyond the confines of rugby and its environs to a global audience of all ages and genders.

The first rugby player in a generation to have a wax figure made of him at the Musée Grévin (the French Madame Tussauds), he was also the face of the company Caron to promote its cologne, "Pour Un Homme", although I should be interested to know what kind of fragrance it actually imparted.

Seb has dressed up as a chambermaid for a 2019 advertising campaign by the hotel chain Marriott, performed The Proclaimers' hit "I'm Gonna Be (500 Miles)", acted as a caveman in a music video promoting the Hong Kong Sevens, and perhaps a high point, dressed up as a "Currency Fairy" for a television advert.

Paris Hilton also recorded a song about him, as if he hadn't suffered enough!

He has launched a clothing range, a wine label, a hotel-restaurant and there was even a Chabal cuddly toy on the market. Also along the way, he managed to find time for a little bit of rugby.

One of the many joys of covering French international rugby is sitting outside a Parisian café on the morning of the match with a strong coffee, a croissant and a copy of the twice- weekly periodical *Midi Olympique*.

A ménage of life's small pleasures rolled into one as you anticipate the upcoming match, study the teams, the players and write a few preparatory notes for post-match articles and reports.

One man who has appeared on the front, middle and back pages of that periodical more than most is Sebastién Chabal.

Just as they used to manufacture boy bands in the Eighties, if you had to manufacture a rugby player in the modern era that would put derrières on seats, provide you with saturation media coverage and sell you a ton of merchandise, then you would create Sebastién Chabal.

His father worked in a garage and his mother in a jewelry shop, so I suppose it was inevitable they would have a child who was showy with a good engine.

Valence is situated in the Drôme department of France on the left bank of the river Rhône.

Known as "The door to the south of France" it is twinned with Clacton-on-Sea, as unlikely a pairing as one might think possible. Clacton might have been Napoleon's favoured invasion point but I can see no synergy between it and the Auvergne-Rhône-Alpes region.

You will notice through this book that I have something of an obsession with the twinning aspect of French and British towns. It never ceases to amaze me how the glamorous French ones get paired up with some tired dreary British counterparts. I'm not sure if there is a dating App for this process, if there is I would suggest the Brits are being somewhat liberal with the truth when compiling their online profile.

A specialty of Valence is the "Suisse," a short crust pastry biscuit in the shape of a man. It contains powdered almond and orange blossom and is the perfect accompaniment to a café crème sitting in the sunshine at Valence's "Maison Nivon" on Avenue Pierre Semard.

Before you think I have morphed into one of the Hairy Bikers, there is a reason why I dwell on this particular delicacy.

My first "Suisse" looked like a representation of one of Valence's finest sons, Sebastién Chabal. With coffee beans for eyes, the pastry version of Chabal bore an uncanny resemblance to the big forward although it would have taken an awful lot of pastry to fully replicate the 17-stone, 6ft 3ins original who has earned a place at lock in my France Hard Man XV.

Seb is a menacing figure. I've always considered him to look like Rasputin on steroids though I certainly wouldn't accuse him of Rasputin's famed lack of grooming. When you meet him in person his sheer size is almost overwhelming. It was frightening enough meeting him in the foyer of the Royal Kensington Hotel, and I can only imagine what a fearsome sight he must have been on the rugby field.

Once the greeting is over and I manage to unclench my buttocks, he gives me a warm smile. My hand disappears in his massive right paw as we shake hands. His deep resonant voice is gentle and has an almost musical quality suggesting that a career in hypnotherapy audio tapes could be a winner.

His menace as well as tenderness were illustrated during the announcement of the host nation for 2023 at the Royal Kensington going from room to room like a hungry bear garnering votes for France's RWC 2023 host nation bid, then minutes later sitting on stage with the late Jonah Lomu's sons, one on each gargantuan knee, tickling them and making funny faces and giggling.

Known as "The Anesthetist" due to his bone-crunching tackles, he didn't take up rugby until the age of 16. He was working in a factory when the Bourgoin coach noticed his massive hands and thought he might have some potential.

He made his international debut against Scotland at Murrayfield in 2000 as a clean-shaven, short-haired 22-year-old, and it was while awaiting the birth of his daughter, Lily Rose, that he started growing his hair and beard. His wife, Annick, insisted that the facial hair remain, and a legend was born.

His caveman image has appealed to men and women alike, but off the field he is a gentle humourous softly-spoken individual and the complete opposite to the rugby-playing persona.

To accompany his massive hands, Chabal has extremely long arms, more Inspector Gadget than Clouseau. Former France prop Christian Califano says: "He's not the only guy I know who can turn the bedroom light off while flat in the bed, but Seb doesn't use the light switch – he unscrews the light bulb!"

In 2007 Chabal made his mark in The Land of the Long White Cloud. France faced the All Blacks at the Westpac Stadium in Wellington and a crunching collision with Ali Williams broke the New Zealander's jaw in several places.

The New Zealand rugby board asked supporters to send in soup recipes to help Williams get the nourishment he needed while he couldn't eat solids.

The endeavor was such a success that a recipe book was published. Chabal says Ali Williams sent him a copy of the book with a note. I haven't been able to discover what the note actually said but I can hazard a guess.

It isn't just opposition players who have been on the receiving end of Chabal's ire. In 2011 he was banned for 60 days for criticizing Top 14 referees. The disciplinary committee ruled the ban would be halved if

Sebastién went on a refereeing course and officiated in three youth team matches!

After four years playing for Bourgoin, he decided to leave the club in 2004. He wanted to join Toulouse, but the club made no approach for him. As a result, former French international and captain, Philippe Saint-André, the director of rugby at Sale Sharks, persuaded him to come to Manchester.

Chabal was primarily a back row player, but France coach Bernard Laporte called him just before the 2007 Rugby World Cup in France to tell him that he wanted to select him for the second row. Seb accepted the offer and became one of the "faces" of a home World Cup.

In September 2007, referee Roy Maybank red-carded him for stamping on former England captain Lawrence Dallaglio during a 16-26 defeat to Wasps. To make matters worse, Chabal appeared to spit at Wasps' Fraser Walters as he trudged off the pitch. A suspension followed for five weeks; two weeks for the stamp and one week for the alleged spit.

Seb used to drive a little red Smart car to training while he was at Sale; he crammed himself into the driver's seat and it was a hugely comical sight with the steering wheel swallowed up into his ample frame. This was the self-deprecating man who endeared himself to everyone at the club.

It was during his time at Sale that he became known as "Seabass", a nickname that replaced "The Caveman" and "The Anesthetist" as he was known in France.

His work rate was criticized at Sale and a club coach from the time revealed that he hated running around the training field. "Others did a lot of work for him but when he rampaged forward or made a big hit, he inspired the whole team. He would get the ball, run through and flatten six people then walk around for two minutes. We knew his weaknesses, but we also knew his strengths."

Kingsley Jones said of Chabal: "You want opponents to be going out a bit fearful, thinking to themselves: 'I don't want to tackle that.'"

He struggled to last a full 80 minutes and was most effective as an impact player coming off the bench for the final 20 minutes. Twenty-six of his 62 international appearances for France came as a replacement.

After five years and 101 appearances in the north of England, Chabal returned to France to join Racing 92 in 2009 where it was reported that he became the highest paid rugby player in the world, earning €1m per year.

In February 2012 after 57 appearances, he left Racing by mutual consent after failing to reach an agreement with club president, Jacky Lorenzetti, on a contract extension and the club's playing strategy moving forward.

The try that showcased the Chabal brand more than any other came at the 2007 Rugby World Cup in the match between France and Namibia in Toulouse. In the white shirt of France (Namibia played in blue) his long sweat-drenched black hair reflected under the floodlights as he took a ball from Frédéric Michalak inside his own half. Chabal drifted outside three Namibians, powered past the full back's attempted tackle on the 22-metre line, then dragged two covering defenders over the try line as he touched down in the right- hand corner.

The crowd went wild, rising to their feet as Chabal made his way back to the halfway line reveling in the adulation. It was one of France's happier moments of a tournament that had a massive high in Cardiff, when France beat the All Blacks, and disappointing lows against Argentina and England.

One of the images of that Rugby World Cup was of Chabal facing the Haka in that quarter final match in Cardiff when France beat the All Blacks.

Chabal liked nothing better than getting in the faces of the opposition and as France slowly marched up to within metres of the Haka, Chabal was there leading the way with his eyes out on stalks. He was the last Frenchman to turn and walk away, still looking over his shoulder and snarling at the All Blacks.

"That quarter final was something special. We beat the All Blacks and it still gives me goose bumps even now" he says.

"We had not planned to react to the Haka the way we did but just before we ran out onto the field, our coaching team told us to act like it was a war so we showed them we were ready to fight."

Those were the days when you were allowed to respond to the Haka, before Rugby World decreed that teams must stand ten metres apart during the war dance.

France tried to encroach in an arrowhead formation at the 2011 Rugby World Cup final against the All Blacks and were fined £2,500 for their trouble.

On 14th December 2013, Lyon faced Agen at home in France's Top 14.

Chabal knocked Marc Giraud unconscious. The Agen player had grabbed hold of his shirt at a maul and Chabal let him have it. He was given a three-week ban. Chabal admitted that he had committed an act of brutality and pleaded guilty. (In light of the television footage showing the act in magnificent close-up, he could do little else.) He apologized and claimed: "It was regrettable, but a reflex action."

At press conferences, Chabal could be extremely moody and menacing. On one occasion ahead of the 2007 Rugby World Cup, he was asked by a journalist if he could respond to a few questions in English. The glare and initial silence gave way to a withering: "No! We are in France, so we speak French." The journalist was wise enough not to pursue the matter any further.

Seb's final French international appearance came against Italy in the Eternal City in the 2011 Six Nations. It was an inglorious ending to the big man's international career as *Les Bleus* fell to a humiliating defeat.

He played 62 times for France; 25 at lock, 23 at number eight and 14 times as a flanker scoring six tries in the process.

In the autumn of 2013, Chabal realized that the passage of time was beginning to catch up with him. He revealed: "I always thought it would be my body and my head that would guide me. My head is not going too badly but my body is suffering. I'm 36 and it becomes hard. Rugby gets complicated so I actually think this will be my last season."

His prediction proved to be accurate and in May 2014 he used a live press conference on *L'Équipe* television to address the nation and announce his retirement at the age of 37.

"I will end my career with pleasure having helped Lyon gain promotion to the Top 14" he said.

The reaction to his statement was incredible. French television ran it as their main story and there was saturation coverage from radio and written media outlets.

Sebastién Chabal was very much rugby's equivalent of Marmite. You either loved him or hated him.

In 2014 the twice-weekly French rugby publication *Midi Olympique* wrote: "Sebastién Chabal will be remembered for a look, some nicknames, some adverts and a little bit of rugby."

In March 2020, while I was in the process of writing this book, Seb was laid low by the Covid-19 virus. He was poorly for a week or so but fortunately he escaped serious damage unlike many of the poor souls who faced him during the 16 years of his colourful and eventful rugby career.

Critics were, and still are, split over Chabal's rugby playing ability but they are totally united in his successful role as a monument to marketing.

Like many players in this book, the public image portrayed was in complete contrast to the private figure.

I will leave the final paragraph of this chapter to Mrs Chabal, Sébastien's wife, Annick.

"When I hear that people imagined that Seb set out to look like Attila the Hun it makes me smile. No one is more sensitive and withdrawn than him."

Chapter 6

Jean-Pierre Rives
"I cannot prevent the French from being French."
Charles de Gaulle

I will never forget the first time I saw Jean-Pierre Rives play in the flesh. It was on 17th February 1979, three days after my nineteenth birthday.

The whole of Northern Europe was engulfed in snow and temperatures were sub-zero.

The Five Nations match between France and Wales was in doubt leading up to the game due to a piece of the roof at Parc des Princes having fallen off as a result of the Siberian weather that had descended on the capital.

Parc des Princes is situated on Rue du Commandant Guilbaud within the affluent 16th (XVIe) arrondissement of Paris, an area that features large museums and the sense of space you get in Kensington or Chelsea. It was once covered with forestry and used for hunting by the French royal family.

The stadium became the home of *Les Bleus* between 1973 and 1977 before they moved to the Stade de France, situated in the commune of Saint-Denis some nine miles north of the city centre. It was a move that sanitized the hostile atmosphere at France home games.

Parc des Princes may have looked like an NCP car park from the outside but within it was a bear pit or bull ring. It was a horrid and intimidating place for opposition teams.

Playing for France that day against Wales, and captaining the side, was a flanker who had taken the rugby world by storm. My excited anticipation at seeing him in the flesh for the first time was overwhelming.

Rives nicknamed Casque d'or (Golden Helmet) or Asterix lit up that dull misty freezing cold day in the French capital. His blond hair shone in the murky darkness of Parc des Princes and he was simply everywhere, racing towards every ruck and maul like a tracer bullet.

At 5ft 10in and 13st 5lb he was not a big man but what he lacked in physique he more than made up for in heart and courage.

"When you're young you're indestructible" says Rives. "You just use your body as a weapon. There were a lot of big guys, and I wasn't very big so I had to find something else." In an amateur era, he would train twice a day, every day, often by himself.

Wales were coming to the end of their golden era in 1979. J. P. R. Williams was still around and captained a new-look Welsh team.

For the record, France won a closely-fought battle 14-13 with the scores level at half-time on seven points apiece.

Jean-François Gourdon scored two tries for France and Aguirre kicked two penalties.

For Wales, Terry Holmes scored a try and Steve Fenwick kicked three penalties.

Jean-Pierre Rives was dabbling in French sporting philosophy long before Eric Cantona's seagulls had located their first trawler.

The maxims have included: "The whole point of rugby is that it is first and foremost a state of mind – a spirit." Other sayings are: "If you want to gain British interest in a war, call it sport. If you want the French to be interested in a sport, call it war." Just two examples from the Rives repertoire.

This rugby philosopher was a vampire's dream. He had the ability to shed a litre of blood from a paper cut, his shirt seemingly permanently covered in the stuff. And when France wore their away strip, the white shirt was regularly covered in more claret than a Bordeaux bar owner's apron.

Jean-Pierre was nailed on for the number six shirt in my French XV. He was fast and creative, an excellent distributor and great support player as well as being an excellent defender. He also proved to be an inspirational captain and great tactician. He would organize the best after-match parties imaginable even if none of us were able to remember a darn thing about them.

Jean-Pierre was born on New Year's Eve 1952 in St. Simon, a village just outside of Toulouse. His mother, Lydia, was Austrian and father Jo was French.

His first love was tennis which combined with a childhood ambition to become a fireman could have taken him far away from the rugby icon that he was to become.

His father made him take up rugby in an attempt to energize him from his relaxed easy- going nature. Rives says the attempt was unsuccessful and that he didn't wake up much!

Many of his international teammates said that half an hour before kick-off Jean-Pierre might be half-asleep in the changing room looking lifeless but once the game kicked off, he flicked a switch and became the human dynamo we all remember.

He studied medicine but dropped out and became a court bailiff before joining the producers of Pastis, Pernod Ricard, doing public relations work which was the kind of role that effectively made him a professional rugby player in an amateur era.

France's observance of amateurism was on a par with Casanova's adherence to celibacy. Players were often courted with job offers, cars and apartments as inducements to join certain rugby clubs.

Rives was offered a job with Pernod Ricard, assisting an executive. When Rives asked what the man he would be shadowing did, he was told: "Nothing. And you can help him do it!"

His move from Toulouse to Racing Club Paris in 1981 ensured that he became the first high-profile French rugby celebrity who would acquire a fame that transcended the sport.

The blond hair, good looks and Corinthian spirit endeared him to a nation that valued and respected style more than substance.

Princess Stéphanie of Monaco and F1 driver Alain Prost were among his famous friends and Rives was one of the guys to be seen with in French society.

The blond bombshell was as hard as nails but rarely violent. He did however lose his cool in a match between his club Toulouse and Avignon in a French league game.

His great friend and fellow flanker for club and country, Jean-Claude Skrela, was flattened by a punch. Rives stepped in and smashed the assailant with a blow that knocked him out cold. Jean-Pierre, being Jean-Pierre, was racked with guilt afterwards and you get the impression that the sense of guilt is still there even after all these years.

Rives may have been only rarely violent but he was brave to the point of foolishness, a trait he shared with an adversary who he respected greatly J. P .R. Williams. The pair had much in common and most obviously the same three initials. Both men appeared to have no regard for their own personal safety.

If there was one game that epitomized Rives' bravery, courage and sheer hardness, it was the second Test between Australia and France in Brisbane on 11th July 1981.

Jean-Pierre had played against New South Wales eight days previously. It was a brutal match during which his right shoulder was smashed by a boot while he was trapped at the bottom of a ruck. As he left the field, the pain of the dislocation seemed almost chiseled across his face.

Jean-Pierre's tour should have been over but with France beset with injuries, he decided he was going to play in the international.

He led France out into the baking Brisbane sunshine, his shoulder hanging in a limp, almost deformed manner that suggested an inhabitant of the 4th arrondissement, the Hunchback of Notre-Dame.

There is no doubt that he shouldn't have been anywhere near the pitch on that day but he played because his country needed him.

Jean-Pierre was unable to tackle or even bind onto the scrum properly and yet he lasted the full 80 minutes, grimacing throughout the game with his face ashen with pain but somehow rocklike as if on Mount Rushmore.

Queensland and Australia flanker Mark Loane (like J. P. R. Williams, a surgeon) said at the time: "It was bravery to the point of insanity."

Rives made his France debut against England aged 22 at Twickenham in 1975.

He simply adored Twickenham. To him it was the cathedral of rugby and making his international debut on the sacred turf was very special.

How did he prepare that nervous night before the game? Early to bed to ensure adequate rest? That was hardly his style, and he was up playing cards until 4 a.m. It certainly didn't appear to do him any harm as France emerged victorious defeating England 27-20.

An international career that consisted of 59 caps would have been much longer had he not had to retire with persistent shoulder problems. Rives captained his country for the first time in his home city, Toulouse, against the USA on 11th November 1978. France won 29-7 in front of a crowd of less than a thousand on Armistice Day and he went on to lead France on 34 occasions which was a world record at the time.

He was part of one of the greatest all-time back rows, not just in France, but across the world stage. When you saw Jean-Pierre Rives, Jean-Claude Skrela and Jean-Pierre Bastiat at 6, 7 and 8 you were in big trouble.

Rives and Skrela struck up a formidable partnership for club and country; the pair became known as Butch Cassidy and the Sundance Kid.

Both were young, handsome and athletic which was of course a dream ticket for every form of media who along with a host of photographers followed them wherever they went.

While they had a telepathic understanding and complemented each other in the jerseys of France and Stade Toulousain, it was a very different story off the field.

Rives was a city slicker who was in his element at parties and night clubs while Skrela was much more of an introvert and enjoyed a more rural existence. They played 25 internationals together for France.

Rives' final international took place at Murrayfield against Scotland in 1984, a match involving two unbeaten teams with a Grand Slam at stake. A sad end to a distinguished career saw Rives become apoplectic with rage as his team were constantly penalized by Welsh referee Winston Jones. "I resented the referee – this setback is already over 30 years old" says Rives. "I prefer to keep my memories to myself."

Jim Telfer, the Scotland coach at the time, said: "After French scrum-half Gallion was taken off injured their confidence took a real dip and it changed the game completely. Rives started mouthing off to the referee and he got on his wrong side."

There is no doubt that Rives' captaincy of France had a galvanizing effect on the team and the style in which it played.

Gareth Edwards, one of Rives' great friends and rivals, says: "France had become very rigid, structured and ill-disciplined in their play. When Jean-Pierre became captain, he gave them flair and discipline and they played their natural game."

"I dreamed all my life of being Gareth Edwards or Phil Bennett or so many of the players I admire like Serge Blanco" says Rives. "But I just played rugby – they played something different. Unfortunately, I didn't have enough talent to play like them but what a pleasure it was to play at the same time as them." This is consummate modesty.

The great All Black number eight Murray Mexted was a victim of Rives' legendary hospitality.

"He's a rugby Napoleon. He was a courageous and outstanding player who has a non-conformist attitude to life."

Mexted recalls: "I remember returning to Paris in 1984 to play for the English Barbarians against the French Barbarians. Rives had organized a party that night but the after-match function lasted for hours and I couldn't leave."

"At about 11 p.m. I finally jumped into a taxi in pursuit of the party venue. I was in a befuddled state. The taxi driver pulled up in a crowded Parisian street and directed me towards a bar that was barricaded by a bouncer. He looked like a gorilla in a suit and he had a cantankerous personality."

"When he heard I was present for Jean-Pierre's party he warmed to me. I was let inside and waiting there were 80 of the most gorgeous women I have ever seen. After midnight, Jean-Pierre and his friends arrive including Graham Mourie. Everything they say that happened on that night actually happened but neither Graham nor I can remember it."

Rives was a friend to the rich and famous with a fanbase stretching across the world and including actor Hugh Jackman. "I was actually pretty obsessed with Jean-Pierre Rives, he was a small guy on the field, but he was as tough as nails and finished every game with blood on his face."

There is one delightful quirky fact that sums up Rives perfectly. After playing a bad game, he would sign all his autographs with a small "r" in his surname. This tiny and seemingly insignificant gesture speaks volumes about the man.

In 1977 Jean-Pierre was chosen to play for the Barbarians against the British Lions at Twickenham in a match organized to celebrate Queen Elizabeth II's silver jubilee.

Playing for the Baa Baas was right up Rives' boulevard; his sporting philosophy was in perfect sync with the club, their ethos and their off-field activities.

The Lions won the match 23-14 with both teams being laden with rugby stars. The blond flanker was in his element. "This game was very special for me … a special spirit."

Following this match, Rives became the guiding light in establishing a French Barbarians team that came to fruition two years later in 1979.

"Creating the French Barbarians was to build a club that reflected the best of rugby and its values of friendship and spirit."

On 14th December 1984, Jean-Pierre Rives announced his retirement at a Paris press conference in typically understated fashion.

"I'm not fit enough to play for my club, Racing, this weekend and not fit for the Five Nations in the New Year, so that's it, goodbye."

Having played against many of the all-time greats, two in particular stood out for Golden Helmet.

"Gareth Edwards was almost impossible to tackle" says Rives. "He is perhaps the greatest player of all time."

All Black captain Graham Mourie became a close friend of the Frenchman and Rives was particularly impressed by how humble the New Zealander had been when France beat the All Blacks 29-14 in the second Test of a two-match series at Eden Park on Bastille Day in 1979.

That match was one of the glory days of French rugby and was a remarkable turnaround after France had lost the first Test 23-9 at Lancaster Park, Christchurch.

Les Bleus scored four tries that day through Caussade, Gallion, Averous and Codorniou. It was their first ever away victory against the All Blacks after eight attempts.

One of Jean-Pierre's current workplaces is a disused railway shed to the north of Paris, the creative home of Rives the sculptor and painter. His works have been exhibited in Paris, Toulouse, Los Angeles and Singapore.

"My success is that I am happy doing it, my ambition is just to go on."

Jean-Pierre emphasizes that art and rugby are one. He talks about the spiritual concept of the team, the glory, the bravery, the sacrifice that the team ethos inspires you to fulfill.

To be the first sculptor since Rodin to be invited to display his work in the Jardin du Luxembourg is impressive to say the least. A Rives "kiss" on the field was less tender than Rodin's famed sculpture of that name.

Jean-Pierre also designed the Giuseppe Garibaldi Trophy which is awarded annually to the winner of the Six Nations match between France and Italy.

As is the way in modern rugby, it appears that every match has to have a trophy.

Rarely seen at rugby matches these days, Rives does not appear to have any yearning for the old life or to marvel at a collection of rugby honours and mementos that his magnificent career allowed him to accumulate.

"Because I am not an African hunter, I do not hunt trophies. I don't want my kids to live in a rugby museum so I gave away most things to my friends – jerseys and things like that."

"That is better because I know they are happy with such things, happier than me, that is for certain."

Life with his second wife, Sonja, and two sons Jasper and Kino-Jean couldn't be better. One of their homes, in St Tropez, is a wooden family property that resembles a tree house.

These days the hair is still blond while the face and waistline are a little fuller. But there is no mistaking the man himself. The body may no longer be up to the rigours of the oval ball game but a look behind the wire-rimmed spectacles reveals those same steely blue eyes that glint with the boldness of the shirt he wore so proudly in the international arena.

As you might imagine, Rives is not particularly enamored of modern rugby and in particular the way coaches call all the shots and the rigid game plans which have the direct result of meaning players are not able, or encouraged, to play what is in front of them. He says: "The players on the field are the bosses so let them decide things.

"We need a revolution. Coaches are imprisoned by the rules, as well as the players, the rules are the enemy."

"You have to be unpredictable, that's what makes it enjoyable otherwise we might as well play the game on an iPad like the kids of today."

It seems appropriate to end this chapter with the words of Rives the philosopher and his take on a sport that now puts its emphasis on size and strength.

"I wonder if even having muscle-bound cheeks is such a good idea. How can you pass the ball if you are unable to smile?"

Chapter 7

Serge Betsen
"Rugby is a wonderful show. Dance, opera and suddenly the blood of a killing."
Richard Burton

"I don't know why, but during the anthem, I see the French flag in front of me and the tears start to flow."
These are the words of Serge Betsen Tchoua, who confesses that he can always be relied upon to become emotional during the singing of "La Marseillaise."

Allons enfants de la Patrie, le jour de gloire est arrivé!
Contre nous de la tyrannie, l'étendard sanglant est levé,
Entendez-vous dans les campagnes, mugir ces féroces soldats?
Ils viennent jusque dans vos bras, egorger vos fils, vos compagnes!
Aux armes, citoyens, Formez vos bataillons,
Marchons, marchons!
Qu'un sang impur, abreuve nos sillons!

As stirring a national anthem as you could wish for and when you hear it sung at the Stade de France, the hairs on the back of the neck stand on end and a shiver goes down the spine. You can even fancy the Eiffel tower is showing its respects as you spot it from the top tiers of the stadium.

Another thing I have noticed is the further south the anthem travels, the more passionate it becomes.

When it gets to the south coast and it swirls and echoes around the Orange Vélodrome in Marseille, with the mountain tops peeking through the gaps in the grandstands, it is an utterly glorious experience.

The temperature also appears to affect the tempo that the anthem is played at.

In Paris it can be slow, but it accelerates the further south it travels so by the time it has reached Marseille, the transformation from "largo" to "allegro" is complete. Lyon would appear to be best place to find a reasonably-paced "Marchons, marchons!"

This wonderful piece of music was written by Claude Joseph Rouget de Lisle in April 1792 in Strasbourg where he was garrisoned during the French Revolutionary Wars.

France had just declared war on Austria and the mayor of Strasbourg held a dinner at which he lamented the fact that France had no national anthem. Rouget de Lisle returned to his quarters and wrote the words in a fit of patriotic ardour. The composition was originally called *Le Chant de guerre pour l'armée du Rhin* ("War Song for the Army of the Rhine"). It was only named *La Marseillaise* after its adoption by the Provençal volunteers who marched into Paris and were prominent in the storming of the Tuileries Palace.

Rouget de Lisle died in poverty in Choisy-le-Roi, his ashes being transferred to Les Invalides in July 1915 as war raged across much of the globe and Italy entered the fray to fight with the Central Powers.

Serge Betsen used to get so would-up and emotional before games that he turned to sophrology, a system of physical and mental exercises whose principal aim is to aid relaxation. He was seeking to control his emotions. "I used to sleep in the dressing room before kick-off to release pressure" he says.

This is a man who always gave everything on the field of play with very little regard for his own safety. More than 200 stitches in his neck and face alone during his playing career pay testament to that. "Pain is something I accept on the pitch" he says.

When your nickname is "Le Secateur" (the Grim Reaper), then it is a reasonable assumption to make that your tackling technique is pretty solid.

Serge Betsen was given this moniker by teammates although this endearingly gentle and amiable man points out that his nickname in French has a slightly different meaning to the English language sense.

"It means, how do you say it … the machine on the farm – the threshing machine. I cut down my opponents' legs like this machine!"

Many rugby players reflect on what it is like to wake up on the morning after an international match and liken the experiences of the day before to having been in a car crash.

I would imagine that waking up the morning after an international match that has seen you play against Serge Betsen would upgrade those sensations to the aftermath of having been in a motorway pile-up.

I consider that Betsen is the perfect foil to Jean-Pierre Rives in my hard man XV; the two players complement each other perfectly and when you see who gets the number eight shirt in the next chapter, I think you'll agree that the back row of this team is going to be a pretty scary outfit.

Serge Betsen's family arrived in Paris on a freezing cold winter's morning in 1983. For his mother and six siblings, it must have seemed a world away from warm and sunny Cameroon. He had been born in 1974 in Kumba, a town that became a trade centre for cocoa and palm oil with most people earning a living as farming families.

Clichy, where the family settled, is historically a working-class multi-ethnic suburb to the north-west of Paris, home to struggling first and second-generation immigrants mainly from Africa. The high-rise estates must have been a dark suffocating presence for the Betsen family.

The suburb became the focus of national and indeed global attention in 2005, when it saw violent protests after two young boys were electrocuted while hiding from police. The protests spread across the nation and France declared its first national state of emergency in 20 years.

Betsen played his first competitive rugby for the local Clichy-based Club Sportif before joining the southern giants Biarritz when he was just 17.

Unlike many flankers, he could play blind and open side of the scrum with equal success. He is also regarded as one of the strongest tacklers in the game and is renowned for his high work-rate on the field.

Jo Maso, the former France national team manager, remembers Serge as a very quiet man. "If you were to tell me he had opened his mouth in the changing room I would be shocked. He prefers to bottle things up but when he does speak, we listen because it is worth listening to."

Maso continues: "He is famous for his tackling, but he is much more than a tackler. He is a superb passer of the ball, and he scores tries."

Betsen made his first appearance for France in 1997 as a replacement against Italy and immediately received a yellow card. He did not receive another call-up until the Six Nations tournament of 2,000 after which he became a regular in the national team.

Coach Bernard Laporte felt Betsen was a bit of a liability and gave away far too many penalties for his liking.

In the Six Nations match against England that year, his relentless man-marking of Jonny Wilkinson resulted in the fly-half being replaced which may have paved the way for a 20-15 French victory.

England's coach, Clive Woodward said of Betsen: "He is the only player that I can say was the single-handed reason we lost a match."

France went on to win the Grand Slam in 2,000 and Betsen was named France's International Player of the Year.

Ex-Scotland fly-half and coach Gregor Townsend says: "Betsen is really quick – he hits you before you have even had time to think. What he is expert at is hitting you legally but just ever so slightly late. Then he holds you down on the ground so you can't get back into the play."

Betsen won the Grand Slam with France in 2002 as part of a wonderful back row together with Olivier Magne and Imanol Harinordoquy.

Fabien Pelous lifted the Six Nations trophy at a sun-drenched Stade de France as *Les Bleus* demolished Ireland 44-5. Betsen showed his attacking credentials that day, scoring two tries in 11 minutes as the men in green were overwhelmed.

Serge was an automatic selection for the 2003 Rugby World Cup and the semi-final loss against England showcased the good, the bad, and the ugly of the Betsen repertoire. He scored an impressive try, but with 52 minutes gone and the match delicately poised at 12-7 to England, Wilkinson cross-kicked to left wing Ben Cohen only to be flattened by a late tackle from Betsen. A yellow card followed, and the 10 minutes spent in the sin bin by the French number 7 changed the course of the match. Wilkinson kicked six points during the sin-binning.

"He [Wilkinson] was lying on the floor for five minutes until the referee gave me a yellow card" says Betsen. "Of course, as soon as I was shown it, he got back up."

"It's true that in these types of games there is big pressure; it's a World Cup semi-final but he was lying on the floor like he's dead. That puts pressure on the referee. When you see the tackle in slow motion it looks much much worse."

"I was in tears after the match because when you work hard you put a lot of sacrifices into the moment, so when it went wrong I had to apologize to my teammates because I was so angry with myself."

England ran out winners 27-7, and another incident in the game resulted in a citing for Betsen after kicking Matt Dawson in the head.

The England scrum-half left the field with blood pouring down his face from the wound and Betsen subsequently received a six-week ban.

Wales and Lions flanker Martyn Williams has huge admiration for Serge and in 2005 described him as the best flanker in the world which is high praise indeed from another truly expert player in this position.

The year 2005 was eventful for Betsen who was cited following an incident during Biarritz's Heineken Cup match against London Wasps in which Wasps' centre Stuart Abbott suffered a broken leg. The complaint was dismissed after a disciplinary hearing found that the trip, while intentional, was not premeditated and had happened in the heat of the moment. He missed the 2005 Autumn Internationals after fracturing his cheekbone playing in a match for Biarritz against Toulouse.

The 2007 Six Nations was won by France, and Betsen played a big part in the success of *Les Bleus*. He completed 56 tackles, 12 more than any other player in the tournament.

Often it was the opposition who suffered at the hands of Betsen but there was one occasion when a couple of well-nourished Welsh brothers turned the tables. He says his most difficult match was against Wales in Cardiff during the 2002 Six Nations. "It was horrendous. I tackled the Quinnell brothers all afternoon – they were huge and they ran at me non-stop. The crowd were f*****g mad."

Towards the end of the 2005 season, Betsen held talks with Leicester Tigers but a possible move from France was aborted when he decided to stay at Biarritz and signed a new three-year contract.

"The Grim Reaper" continued his global tackling extravaganza on the international stage and the 30 tackles he made during the Wales vs France match in 2007 set a world record for an international rugby match at the time.

After being selected as a member of the France squad for the 2007 Rugby World Cup, with France as hosts, he missed out on the majority of one of *Les Bleus'* greatest matches when they defeated the All Blacks in a breathtaking quarter final at the Millennium Stadium.

Betsen only lasted four minutes and 32 seconds of the match after being concussed while attempting to tackle Joe Rokocoko. Having got his head on the wrong side, Rokocoko's hip bone struck Betsen. As he went down, Fabian Pelous' knee made contact with his head.

As Betsen lay motionless there was great concern for his safety and the medics ran onto the field to get him on his side and remove his gum shield.

Fortunately, Serge was able, eventually, to get to his feet and stagger off to watch the rest of the famous victory on television in the medical room.

France once again proved to be New Zealand's bogey team, and after making 200 tackles that night *Les Bleus* emerged victorious 20-18.

Yannick Jauzion's winning try still grates with the All Blacks, as English referee Wayne Barnes failed to spot a forward pass in the build-up, an error that resulted in a urinal in the Cowboy bar in Searle Lane, Queenstown, New Zealand, being fitted out with a bust of the Englishman, no doubt to improve the aim of the male customers. There is also another urinal of a similar nature "dedicated" to journalist, rugby writer and my dear friend Stephen Jones of *The Sunday Times*.

A brain scan was conducted following Betsen's injury after which he self- deprecatingly pointed to the centre of his forehead and said: "There's nothing in there anyway, I'm fine!"

He recovered in time to play in the semi-final defeat in Paris to England, a match that he describes as one of the biggest regrets of his life, along with the other semi-final defeat to England in 2003.

On 16th January 2008, Betsen announced that he was retiring from international rugby with immediate effect. Four months later it was revealed that he had signed for the English club Wasps.

The move from Biarritz to Ealing must have been quite a culture shock following 12 years and 172 appearances for the Atlantic coast outfit.

"I was really surprised by how little talk there was in the dressing room – so different to France" he says.

Betsen made a good start with Wasps, performing well and earning respect from the Wasps supporters. He played for the 'A' side while recovering from injury before moving into the first XV. During the 2009 Six Nations championship he was made Wasps' captain in the absence of the senior England players. (His friend Rafa Ibañez was also unavailable having been forced into retirement by injury.) The club announced that he would share the captaincy for the remainder of the 2008/09 season with Phil Vickery. Betsen left Wasps in June 2011 and announced his retirement from rugby at his "Jubilee" game in Biarritz on 6th June 2012.

Betsen was a trailblazer for the small wave of African-born players who have played for France. He suffered from racism but refuses to dwell on that. "My play frustrated opposition players and they responded stupidly. I never said anything back and just concentrated on the game."

"My success as a player was down to my mentality to be the best player I could be. I had to work really hard because it's not just about talent."

His most difficult opponent was All Black Richie McCaw, and Betsen was one of very few people who achieved more wins than losses when he played against the legendary New Zealander.

"Richie was my toughest opponent but I was able to beat the All Blacks twice in the three times I played against them, and I felt I got the better of him when we faced each other."

These days, the softly spoken number seven is kept busy with the Serge Betsen Academy and his work with Peace and Sport ("L'Organisation pour la Paix par le Sport".)

When he returned to his homeland in 2001, he saw youngsters playing rugby in the Biyem-Assi de Yaoundé district of Cameroon. The club had 15 registered players and when he returned to France, Betsen set up his academy supporting children from underprivileged backgrounds to enable them to play rugby.

In 2017 when Betsen was awarded the Légion d'honneur at the French embassy in London, the French ambassador had this to say: "Rugby is a sport that requires commitment. Players have to be brave and surpass themselves through an ability to overcome suffering and be constantly active on the pitch."

"These days the emotions are still there for me when La Marseillaise rings out at rugby grounds around the world" says Serge Betsen and that's just as it should be.

Arise children of the country, the day of glory has arrived

Against us the bloodied banner of tyranny is raised

Do you hear in the countryside, the roar of those ferocious soldiers?

They come right here among us to cut the throats of your sons and your women

To arms citizens, form your battalions

Let's march let's march

Let an impure blood water our furrows.

Chapter 8

Chapter 8

Marc Cécillon
"France has neither winter nor summer nor morals. Apart from these drawbacks it is a fine country."
Mark Twain

Depression, alcoholism and prison. Life after rugby for Marc Cécillon was not the idyll he would have hoped for.

Sport can be a cruel mistress; there are many great athletes who have found life after retirement almost suffocatingly impossible to cope with. Cricket and boxing are the prime examples but rugby is no exception to this curse.

Even in today's more enlightened and mental-health-aware society, the transition between the sporting world and the more mundane one that the rest of us inhabit can be a rocky, lonely and perilous path.

Fortunately, the modern professional game has organizations and protocols in place that will guide rugby players through this difficult chapter of their lives. Attitudes are slowly changing and there is certainly a more open conversation about depression and mental health problems.

Not so long ago, and particularly in the macho world of French rugby, the answers to problems of this nature were looked for in a bottle. Drinking to forget and to dull the pain was the order of the day. As for talking to your teammates and friends about your issues, well that would have been well beyond the pale.

Many players have travelled this torturous route, but few will have had to endure their agonies under intense media spotlight and such public scrutiny.

Marc Cécillon was an ordinary down to earth man who just happened to be good at rugby and his tale demonstrates just how far an athlete can fall from grace.

Life after retiring from the game spiraled out of control, lurching from one disaster to another. Cries for help were not forthcoming from a proud strong man and even though the signs of his turmoil were evident to others, no one appeared to reach out a hand to stop him from drowning.

However, he gets a starting place in this exclusive XV as a number eight who straddled the amateur and professional eras. At 6ft 3in and just over 18 stone, his physical attributes as well as a mobility that belied his size constituted a huge plus.

His ability to play lock, flanker and number eight with equal aplomb is also an asset to any team. A creative and skillful ball-carrier, he created space for others by drawing in tacklers. And as a good reader of the game, Cécillon could be relied on to choose the right option at the base of the scrum. He knew whether to pass or pick and go. He was also always eager to get his hands on the ball, whether in attack or defence, and of course his brutal tackling was another string to an impressive bow.

From first minute to last, "Marco" would give you everything. He would empty the tank and even then, he'd give you the fumes from the tank.

Marc Cécillon's life story has filled the front and back pages of *Le Monde* and *L'Equipe*, and every other conceivable media outlet. The sad fact is that a wonderful rugby player will forever be remembered for the tragedy and the misery he inflicted on his family, and indeed on himself, rather than for being a very special and outstanding rugby player.

Here was a man who appeared to have everything; the striking good looks of a Roman warrior and a beautiful wife with two lovely daughters. He reached the highest peak of his sport, playing 46 times for France between 1988 and

1985 including five matches as captain. He was a hard tough man, a strong ball carrier and an abrasive tackler who never took a backward step.

His first cap came on 20th February 1988 against Ireland at Parc des Princes in front of 49,000 in round three of the Five Nations Championship, a match in which France were victorious by 25 points to 6.

France scored five tries that day through Philippe Sella, Didier Camberabero, Alain Carminati, Patrice Lagisquet and Serge Blanco. Philippe Bérot landed one conversion and Camberabero slotted a drop goal. Ireland's points came from two Michael Kiernan penalties.

Playing first division rugby for Bourgoin at the age of 17 gives an indication of just how tough and talented Mark Cécillon was. The rugby served up those days in France was not for the faint-hearted, and to wear the CS Bourgoin-Jallieu shirt so proudly for 23 years is quite an achievement.

His final international appearance was so very nearly in the 1995 Rugby World Cup final in Johannesburg, an act that would have denied us all those emotional iconic moments when Nelson Mandela, wearing a Springbok number six shirt, presented the Rugby World Cup to South Africa captain Francois Pienaar. Strangely enough, it was a Welshman who played a vital role that enabled South Africa to reach that famous final.

The city of Durban has a reputation for its glorious weather, but 17th June 1995 proved an exception.

The heavens above Kings Park opened shortly before kick-off, producing extraordinary rainfall that left the pitch waterlogged.

The start was delayed as ground staff, cleaners, ball boys and every other available employee, worked at a frenetic pace to push the surface water off the pitch. They used brushes, brooms, mops, squeegees and buckets, in fact everything but the kitchen sink. Actually, maybe the kitchen sink in hindsight would have been quite useful.

The match referee was Derek Bevan of Wales, and he would prove to be a pivotal figure in proceedings that day.

His main concern ahead of kick-off was the danger of a scrum collapsing in one of the large pools of water on the pitch.

If the match had been called off, the Springboks would have been eliminated under the tournament rules due to their disciplinary record in the pool stages, and as a result France with would have progressed to the final.

The game eventually got underway, but the rain returned, turning the match into a lottery with the contest being dominated by kicking and handling errors.

Both France and the Springboks tried to keep the game as tight as possible but that proved virtually impossible.

France peppered the Boks' back three with high kicks that caused them all sorts of trouble in the appalling conditions.

The Springboks scrum was dominant even in the wet, and they showed remarkable control to drive the French eight back from five metres out, allowing Ruben Kruger to dive onto the ball to score.

The Boks established a 10-0 lead, but France found a way back through the boot of their number 10 Thierry Lacroix who kicked five penalty goals. South African fly-half Joel Stransky landed four penalties as well as converting Kruger's try.

As the game reached a tense and nervous finale, France thought they had scored a match- wining try. Full-back André Joubert spilled a high ball and Abdel Benazzi came barreling in to gather the low ball and dive for the line. James Small provided a vital intervention; showing no regard for his own safety he bravely used his body to block the Frenchman from going over. Benazzi maintains he got over, but referee Derek Bevan ruled no try.

So, Marc Cécillon's international career came to a disappointing end on a dank night in KwaZulu-Natal

73

Province as the Springboks clung on in the dying minutes to emerge victorious 19-15.

I'm sure you don't need reminding that the Boks went on to beat New Zealand in the final and lifted the Rugby World Cup at their first attempt.

After 46 French caps of which 31 were on the winning side, and one drawn match, Cécillon's international career came to an end although he continued to play club rugby for Bourgoin-Jallieu for another four years before retiring in 1999.

Marc was not especially noted for on-field thuggery but he did have his moments.

Peter Wright the Scotland prop takes up the story: "At the 1995 Rugby World Cup in South Africa, I was rucking and managed to rake the shirt off French fly-half Thierry Lacroix's back as he lay prone on the floor. I was standing there looking smugly at my efforts when Marc Cécillon came flying across the ruck and smashed me in the jaw. He wasn't the kind of bloke you messed with, although I did spend the rest of the match trying to get even."

Marc Cécillon was known as "The quiet man of French rugby", a very shy and reserved character, he hesitated to accept the French captaincy due to the nerve-racking media duties involved. After only five matches in charge, he resigned from the captaincy.

He made clear the reasons for his resignation. "The pressure of the press was hard to take, and I was afraid of expending all my energy before kick-off, and of not being the same player on the field. I couldn't stand making speeches at banquets."

Cécillon was worshiped and adored in Bourgoin-Jallieu, his hometown in the foothills of the Alps, a place that gave birth to the wonderful Chaudelet galette, a small savoury short-crust pastry flavoured with aniseed.

If Marc Cécillon was the "God" of Bourgoin-Jallieu, then his replacement on the bench would surely be a baker-cum-priest called Pitrougnard, the man who invented the Chaudelet at the end of the nineteenth century.

It is said in these parts that Pitrougnard kneaded the dough with his feet and sold the pastries on the platforms of Bourgoin station singing: "They are hot the pots, they are hot!" His sales pitch may not have been outstanding, but as the saying goes, the proof of the pudding is in the eating. Purely in the spirit of journalistic enquiry I felt obliged to road- test a fair quantity of these delicacies and I'm more than happy to give them my personal endorsement.

Incidentally, Bourgoin-Jallieu has a somewhat unlikely twin town in the form of Dunstable, the Bedfordshire market town cradled by the Chilterns which produced Hollywood star Gary Cooper, an actor who played many gun-slinging roles in the magnificent Westerns that were all the rage when I was a boy. For reasons that will become clear later, there is a certain irony to this twinning connection.

The village of Saint-Savin is located on the left bank of the Gartempe river, it is a small community noted for its abbey which is a UNESCO world heritage site. The most notable event for the locals is the weekly Friday morning market. But in this sleepy town on 7th August 2014, the lives of Marc Cécillon and his family were about to change for ever.

A barbecue at the villa of his best friends, Christian and Babeth Beguy, was intended to be a warm friendly evening for 60 or so guests.

Chantel Cécillon, a medical secretary who married Marc when she was 17, arrived on time without her husband and was sitting at a table with some female friends.

Marc had spent the afternoon riding his Harley-Davidson and when he arrived at 11 p.m. he was drunk. Madame Beguy tried to persuade him to eat some food and he apparently grumbled before hitting her in the face causing a black eye.

Cécillon was thrown out of the party but was spotted by the hosts' teenage son, a little while later, walking back up the driveway while tucking a .357 magnum revolver into his shorts, a gun he had obtained during a rugby tour to South Africa in 1992.

The teenager attempted to warn as many guests as possible and ushered them to the lower part of the garden. But Cécillon headed straight towards his wife and shot her four times in the arm, chest and head.

Guests tried to overpower him, and one threw a concrete block which hit him on the back but made no impression. Eventually several guests restrained Cécillon and tied him to a chair with electrical cord.

The gendarmerie arrived and Cécillon appeared astounded when they told him he had killed his wife. "That's not possible" he shouted. "I love her."

Toxicology reports stated there were 2.35 grams per litre, nearly five times the legal limit of alcohol, in his blood. He did not fully comprehend what had happened until he sobered up in his cell the following day.

The five-day trial began on 5th November 2006 at the Grenoble Criminal Court. Cécillon arrived handcuffed wearing a stylish suit for this case which was unsurprisingly to make big news and receive massive coverage to feed the interest of an eager French public.

The jury of five women and four men heard how Cécillon had been depressed after retiring as a sporting icon and returning to ordinary life.

Psychiatric reports submitted to the court revealed a fragile personality in a depressed state. He was also described as suffering a frenzy of passionate jealousy regarding his wife.

Under cross-examination, the former France international stated that he loved his wife, but they often argued after she had revealed her intention of leaving him. Two weeks before being killed she had started divorce proceedings.

Cécillon had previously told investigators that he thought his wife was being unfaithful and he only wanted to intimidate her.

He told the court: "I admit today that I fell into alcoholism while being totally absorbed in my own little bubble. I exploded and I don't know why. I always loved my wife and I always will. I only wanted to intimidate Chantel not kill her."

Cécillon admitted shooting his wife but denied murder. His lawyer argued that the incident occurred while the accused was in a state of depression following his retirement as a top sportsman.

The accused told the court: "I should have spoken up, I realize this because of the 27 months I have spent in prison before this trial, which has allowed me to work on myself. I turned in on myself too much, perhaps I turned too much to alcohol and used it to escape."

Family members burst into tears when he described his inability to talk about his difficulties.

Prosecutor Françoise Pavan-Dubois said Cécillon had not acted on the spur of the moment but had planned to kill his wife, also stating that he had fired the gun into his ceiling at home to test it before returning to the party.

Cécillon refuted the accusations and said: "I wanted my wife to come home with me, I wanted the two of us to leave together. Why did I shoot? It is a question I shall ask myself all my life. I didn't plan anything. I wish I could understand."

"I ask for pardon from my wife Chantel, I loved her, pardon from my daughters Angelique and Celine, pardon from my mother-in- law Marinette. I never thought I'd do it," he said before breaking down in floods of tears.

His daughters Angelique and Celine, who appeared as co-plaintiffs, told the court their father's alcoholism had turned family life into a living nightmare.

"Why did you do this to us? I will never forgive you, I no longer have a mother" shouted Celine, fixing her father in the eyes on the second day of the trial. Her sister Angelique burst into tears while addressing him. "I will never forgive you even if I love you."

Cécillon's close friend and international colleague Jean-François Tordo described to the court the events that led up to the fateful shooting.

"Marc was on his Harley, he dropped by for a coffee and stayed for about two and a half hours. We had played boules the night before and he wanted to stay on and play some more. He did not want to go to the party."

"Marco was always being invited for drinks and to parties, it looked good for the hosts if they had him as a guest so they could brag if they had spent an afternoon with him. He couldn't say no but he found it a burden to be in such demand."

"He was a man with no limits; he did everything with a passion. In a way I think there was love in what he did, in killing her I mean, at least there wasn't evil. I think what happened was the result of an accumulation of years of unexpressed emotions. He needed affection; he needed his friends. But equally he did not show his emotions. He was this giant iceberg and we only saw the tip of him. As a friend, I feel I should have been more sensitive to the pain under the surface."

Tordo who had been a friend for 15 years played 15 times for France between 1991 and 1993 as a flanker, number eight and hooker.

Pascale, Tordo's wife, gave a different perspective on Cécillon. "He was a drunk, he drank, he screwed and he always got away with it because he was Marc Cécillon. That is what 20 years of alcohol does to you – little by little it destroys you. Marc could not cope with life. When you kill your wife, you are killing your life."

Longtime friend Gilles told *Le Parisien* newspaper: "We knew he was in a bad way, but we never imagined such a thing happening. He cut himself off from his friends. We should have done more."

Another friend, Serge Adler, went on to say: "After the honours and the glory, he returned to a simpler life. He found himself left to his own devices and sank into a deep depression."

Along with Serge Blanco, other French sporting stars were called as witnesses including the President of the French Rugby Federation at that time, Bernard Lapasset.

Prosecutor Pavan-Dubois described Cécillon as a violent sexually-obsessed man who had made life hell for his wife and daughters, and a man who had been unable to accept coming down from his pedestal as a star player.

Summing up, defence lawyer Paul-Richard Zelmati told the court: "It's a simple story of a crime of passion committed through alcohol and depression. All he knew in his life was how to play rugby.

"He's a simple country man who has realized the magnitude of what he has done, and is suffering a lot because of it, and is terribly ashamed."

Marc's daughter Angelique made an emotional plea to the jury. "I don't think my father intended to kill my mother," she said, begging the jury to show clemency. She pleaded that she missed both her parents and that her father had already been punished enough.

The jury were asked to decide whether Marc Cécillon had committed premeditated murder, which carries a mandatory life sentence, or involuntary manslaughter for which the sentence can be as low as three years.

On 10th November 2006, Cécillon was charged with premeditated murder and given a 20- year sentence, five years longer than the prosecution had asked for.

Bourgoin club chairman Pierre Martinet said: "I have known Marc for 12 years. I often saw him with Chantal who was very proud of him. I never noticed problems between them, and I never personally saw him drunk. But it is clear that his recent lack of activity tended to incite him to drink."

Sensing Cécillon was struggling with life as an ex-player, Martinet appointed him honorary manager of Bourgoin and put him in charge of selling corporate VIP suites at the club's stadium.

"No one can save another man," said Martinet. "If those of us who knew Marc put our hands to our hearts, we have to admit there were problems with alcohol and giving up playing. But no one had the full story. No one really knew what went on at home. It is too easy to be wise after the event."

Some two years later, on 3rd December 2008, the 20-year sentence was reduced on appeal to 14 years. Appeal court judge Marie-Claude Berenger decided the killing had not been premeditated. Cécillon's mother-in-law and daughters played a major role in getting the sentence reduced and his exemplary behaviour while being behind bars also counted in his favour.

Another casualty from the fall-out of the murder trial was Alexandre Dumoulin, the Racing Metro (now known as Racing 92) and French international centre who revealed during a 2015 Six Nations training camp that Marc Cécillon was his biological father.

Alexandre, the eight-times capped France centre, was only told the news prior to the murder trial.

Before the trial, his mother Carole Dumoulin said: "I was 19 years old. I had an adventure with Marc, I was simply in love." She continued her testimony with: "I had a child, Alexandre, who was recognized by another, but

Marc Cécillon is the parent. He was married, I did not ask him to recognize the child. I respected his choice of life."

Throughout his career, Alexandre Dumoulin has never sought to meet Marc Cécillon. "For him, there was no 'before and after' the day he learned it," says his agent. There was never a physical meeting between them, nor an attempt. No texting, no email either. But that doesn't mean they'll never meet." The Racing player takes advantage of free weekends to go to see his mother and his stepfather whom he calls Xav in Villefranche-sur-Saône in the Rhône department.

More problems followed in 2018 when Cécillon was charged with drink-driving, driving without a valid license, speeding, violence and theft.

While working at a vineyard and drinking during a harvesting event, he reportedly assaulted the vineyard's owner then got into a vehicle before crashing it into a parked truck.

His lawyer Youssouf Sow told the court "He does not drink very often but when he does, he doesn't know how to stop."

A judge in Perpignan sentenced Cécillon to twelve months in prison, six months of which were suspended. At the trial, Marc acknowledged that he was still struggling with alcohol and the court ordered him to seek treatment.

Cécillon now lives in the beautiful little town of Collioure, the pearl of the Vermilion coast and just a few kilometers from the Spanish border. It's a town where artists came to depict the glorious shades of light and unusual landscapes that nature has bestowed on this picture postcard of a location.

Matisse, Picasso and Salvador Dali frequented Collioure in the early 1900s, no doubt sampling the local Grenache and Syrah grapes and the refreshing raspberry-coloured aromatic Rose.

Since his parole Marc has set up home here with his new partner. A new life perhaps but the fact that he spent many carefree summers in Collioure with his daughters when they were young children means the memories live on.

The events of that humid August night, and all that followed, made it impossible for Marc to return to the Bourgoin-Jallieu region. The vines on the hillsides of Roussillonnais remind him of home says a friend who has remained loyal to him.

Here on the edge of the Mediterranean, among the coloured facades, café terraces and the small, pebbled beaches, maybe Marc Cécillon can find inspiration from the words of Jean-Paul Sartre: "Life begins on the other side of despair."

Chapter 9

Philippe Carbonneau
"If you can't take a punch, you should play table tennis."
Pierre Berbizier

If a rugby player epitomizes a town and a rugby club, then Phillipe Carbonneau, my selection at scrum-half, is that man.

Brive-la-Gaillarde in the Corrèze department is a proper rugby town. When you play their team you play the whole town – not just the whole town but also its history, culture, present and even future.

This delightful medieval sub-prefecture was a regional capital of the French Resistance in World War Two and was the first city of occupied France to liberate itself by its own means in 1944. So it knows a thing or two about conflict and self-determination. It lies along the Corrèze river west of the Massif Central in the Nouvelle-Aquitaine region.

You could not wish for a more welcoming and friendly atmosphere as you sip your café crème watching the world go by, sitting outside one of the many authentic bars and cafes in Place Latreille or Rue du Lyon.

An exception to this rule is visiting rugby teams who are viewed with deep suspicion and regarded as an enemy that have come to steal the town's pride and besmirch its honour.

The inherent culture of French rugby is the major factor of this ambience, a culture that has been centered on winning games at home, while on the other side of the coin, away games were treated as an annoying but necessary inconvenience.

L'esprit de clocher is the phrase that defines this rugby culture, being translated as "the spirit of the bell tower." It meant that you simply do not lose a rugby match within the sound of your own church bells.

Rugby became popular in the south-west of France as a form of regional identity and as a form of defiance against Paris who were trying to stamp out local culture. There was also a time when the Catholic church in France thought playing rugby was a sin. They considered it too violent and found the proximity of male bodies unpalatable and even sinful.

Many town dignitaries supported and encouraged rugby purely because of the stance taken by the church, and this is where the game grew as a symbol of local pride.

Matches became a way of settling local feuds that had existed for centuries, and with the players coming from mostly agricultural backgrounds, the farms and vineyards were a conveyor belt of talent.

Rugby values had not been invented or considered as referees were regularly beaten up and teams would poach opposition players with financial and material inducements. An 18- year-old boy was killed by a high tackle from a French international in a championship semi-final. It was a long way from "jouer jouer" which is sometimes translated in English circles as carefree "chuckabout" rugby.

The Basques and Catalans of the area were ideally suited to the game and the way it was being played in these parts. This was a style that was a world away from the open running version being played up north in Paris.

Club Athlétique Brive Corrèze Limousin, to give the team its full title, was founded in 1910, and before the Second World War it switched to rugby league but returned to union when the war ended.

Brive have constantly provided players for the national team including Amédée Domenech nicknamed "Le Duc" ("The Duke") who played there in the Fifties and Sixties and gave his name to the stadium shortly after his death in 2003.

Other great names to have represented Brive are France flanker Olivier Magne, fly-half Alain Penaud, and number eight Jean-Luc Joinel.

The club have also fielded internationals of a global nature, Argentina's Lisandro Arbizu (one of the first from his country to migrate to Europe) and his compatriot prop Christian Martin also played for them, as have Pacific Islanders Norman Ligairi of Fiji, Samoan Terry Fanolua and Suka Hufanga of Tonga.

Home nations representatives include Barry Davies of Wales, Andy Goode and Ben Cohen of England and Gregor Townsend, Mike Blair and Tom Smith of Scotland.

Jacques Chirac, the French President from 1995-2007, also played for Brive's youth team at number 8 and second row. You have to wonder if Chirac and Bill Clinton ever discussed rugby, the latter having been a squad member and a "rather lumpy but excellent" second row for Little Rock (Arkansas) R.F.C. and known to play occasionally while at Oxford.

Another Welsh international, Derwyn Jones, recalls playing for Brive as a 41-year-old in the French second division.

"I couldn't believe it, my teammates were headbutting each other before kick-off!" I remember one of my first games for Brive, Andy Goode, the Englishman was at fly-half, and as he lined up to take a penalty, the crowd – all 20,000 of them – started humming 'God Save The Queen!'"

Townsend, Scotland's mercurial fly-half, joined Brive in 1998 and couldn't believe his eyes when he arrived there to see coach Laurent Seigne fighting with his own forwards before a game.

Brive and Pontypridd were drawn in the same pool at the 1997/98 Heineken Cup tournament, and it was inevitable that the match in France would be tasty. As it turned out, it was one of the darkest days in Brive's rugby history.

Now if there is one team you didn't mess with, it was Pontypridd. They weren't called the "Valley Commandos" for their inherent tenderness and warmth of spirit. Their home ground, Sardis Road, was known as the "House of Pain," and it never failed to deliver on the threat in the nickname. This was a tough Welsh valley town that also lived and breathed rugby; it was Brive without the sunshine and les escargots.

"Ponty" is one of those places that is hard to describe to anyone who hasn't been there or is not Welsh.

The town is situated at the meeting point of two rivers, the Rhondda and the Taff. It was once described by playwright and novelist Gwyn Thomas as "the Damascus of the valleys". It has also held an unusual record of having the longest station platform in the world.

Pontypridd and Brive have a lot in common; they are both small, close-knit, fiercely proud and harbour a feeling that sometimes the world is against them.

Brive scrum half Philippe Carbonneau joined the club after winning the inaugural Heineken Cup with Toulouse in 1996 and in that final he played alongside his brother, Olivier, in a pulsating game against Cardiff at the old Cardiff Arms Park.

Toulouse won 21-18 after extra time having scored two tries in the opening ten minutes through Castaignède and Cazalbou but Adrian Davies' boot kept Cardiff in the hunt.

The French outfit led 15-12 as the match entered stoppage time and a last-gasp Davies penalty took matters into extra time.

Davies and Deylaud exchanged penalties, and with only seconds remaining Cardiff were penalized for handling in the ruck so allowing Deylaud to slot home a kick to win the trophy.

Carbonneau was made captain of Brive on his arrival from Toulouse and despite being a timid character off the field, he had a reputation for being a hot-headed impulsive individual on it.

A scrum-half is usually a small person with a big voice and some serious psychological issues, a personality that allows them to bark like one of those small yappy dogs while thinking they are an Alsatian.

It is also said that a scrum-half doesn't shy away from a scrap and starts them more frequently than anyone else on the team. Philippe Carbonneau epitomizes these qualities.

Born in Toulouse on 15th April 1971 and standing at 5ft 7in, what he lacked in height he made up for in attitude. He gained 33 international caps for France, scored five tries and won two Grand Slams with *Les Bleus* in 1997 and 1998.

His international debut came in 1995 against Romania in the Latin Cup in Argentina, where France were victorious 52-8. Thomas Castaignède, Fabien Pelous and Olivier Azam also made their French debuts that day.

France scored seven tries through Carminati, Castaignède, Delaigue, Lièvremont, Pelous and Arlettaz (two).

Philippe's club career started at Toulouse and ended in Tarbes with Brive, Pau and Dax coming in between.

To say that Carbonneau had a short fuse would confound the gauges of every explosive expert on the planet. For club and country, he would often be the catalyst for mass brawls and punch-ups. He was particularly aggressive, the headbutt being his weapon of choice.

But he was aware of his deficiencies and once told a local newspaper journalist: "I know I have a lot of defects – that's perhaps why I have been made captain of Brive. I have a tendency to talk back to referees, but I am trying hard to correct myself and be calmer on the field of play."

Carbonneau's scrum-half skills were not up to scratch when he arrived at Brive but with the World Cup-winning Australian number nine, Nick Farr-Jones at the club as a technical advisor, rapid improvements were made to his game.

However, his hard man image took a dent from which he never recovered when at Parc des Princes in 1997, Arwel Thomas the Welsh fly-half laid him out with a right hook leaving the French scrum-half flat on his panties.

Arwel was eleven stone dripping wet and you would find more meat on a butcher's pencil. But Carbonneau's fearsome reputation was laid to waste on the lush sunlit Parisian turf that spring day.

"He pushed me under my chin" said Arwel. "He was in my face, I just reacted and punched him in the face. Straight away I thought I might be sent off. The incident was replayed and the crowd gasped. I thought: 'This is it!'"

"Really, I should have been sent off. If you punch someone in the face you should not stay on the field."

"Six years later [in 2003] I joined the French club Pau and one of the first people I met was my old sparring partner Philippe Carbonneau!

"He ended up being my captain when I played there. We had some stick initially, but they made us training partners. I got really friendly with him and his family – he was a brilliant player, one of the best I ever played with or against."

But back to 14th September 1977 and a Heineken Cup match that will go down in sporting annals for all the wrong reasons. Three Brive players ended up in hospital and four Pontypridd players in court!

Carbonneau, unsurprisingly, was involved in almost everything unsavoury that occurred on and off the field that day in one of the most ugly and ill-tempered matches in rugby history.

Brive were the European champions at the time, having beaten Leicester 28-9 in the final in Cardiff the previous season.

No one gave Pontypridd a chance in Brive; all the other sides that had gone out there previously had been blown away and there was an aura of invincibility about the French teams at that time.

Pontypridd knew exactly what to expect. They had already played at Dax that season and team manager Eddie Jones sent out a message to Brive leading up to the game saying that his side: "… had the bottle for it. We don't intimidate easily which is what French sides like to do."

The red rags and bulls scenario was well and truly set.

Brive were a fearsome force on and off the field with the home fans making the Parc Municipal des Sports a scary place to play.

Even in the tunnel before kick-off, Brive started to verbally wind up the opposition with some Gallic gestures thrown in for good measure.

The match began with both teams fired up to the hilt. Ponty took an early lead and Brive were beginning to look a bit rattled. After about 20 minutes, following a scrum on the Pontypridd try lines, Dale McIntosh was pinned on the ground with French fists pummeling him from all sides.

Martyn Williams recalls being first on the scene and grabbing McIntosh's arms in an attempt to pull him away, but his actions just made matters worse because the big New Zealander couldn't defend himself. Within a matter of seconds, it turned into a mass brawl with even diminutive wing Gareth Wyatt being involved. Carbonneau was in his natural habitat – in the thick of the mayhem.

The Pontypridd players I have spoken to since the event remain astounded that Carbonneau didn't get sent off that day after punching, gouging, use of his knees plus a trademark headbutt all of which could been seen on live television.

Carbonneau does now admit to the headbutt, but I don't think he asked for all his other offences to be taken into account.

When the fighting subsided, referee Ed Murray red-carded Dale McIntosh along with French international flanker Lionel Mallier. As McIntosh walked off, he gave a thumbs-up sign to the crowd which inflamed matters.

Some rugby broke out in between the fighting, and after going ahead through tries by Dafydd James and Kevin Morgan, Ponty lost the match 32-31 with the controversy continuing to the bitter end when Brive were awarded a try that could be described as dubious at best.

Brive had played Welsh sides at home in the previous season. Their intimidation had worked, and they had got away with it so they couldn't quite believe it when Pontypridd gave as good as they got.

After the final whistle, the Brive players invited the Pontypridd visitors and officials to a local bar to bury the hatchet. Unfortunately, it was almost the literal meaning of that phrase that took place.

Le Bar Toulzac is typically French. It is set in a peaceful square and a soothing fountain greets you at 8 Place des Patriotes Martyrs.

A blackboard on legs listed the day's "specials" but for the Brive and Pontypridd players there turned out be plenty of afters.

The bar was owned by a couple of former Brive players, and the atmosphere was initially convivial with players and their family members present. Neil Jenkins was having a friendly chat with a few of the French players, including French international centre Christophe Lamaison.

All of a sudden, the bar resembled a scene from a Wild West movie, with bottles and chairs flying everywhere. Jenkins took his wife and her family outside the bar away from danger before returning inside to locate Dale McIntosh. Both Jenkins and McIntosh had court cases pending following a previous night club incident so the last thing either of them needed was more trouble.

Once again Carbonneau was to be found at the source of the incident, apparently winding up Phil John (not the wisest of moves) and while that exchange appeared to calm down, a fracas developed in the corner of the bar after a bottle was thrown. The bottle hit Jason Lewis causing all hell to break loose and a fight erupted throughout the bar. La gendarmerie were called and launched themselves into the bar firing tear gas and dishing out some pretty rough treatment of their own.

David Venditti, the Brive and France winger, had a take on the story. "I was talking with Neil Jenkins when I saw that McIntosh and Phil John were threatening Carbonneau. I asked Jenks to calm them down, but it was too late – they were fighting already. Lamaison got a chair in the face and Carbonneau was hit by broken glass. When the police arrived, my shirt had gone and I was bleeding all over."

Pontypridd's players went back to their hotel where team doctor Dave Pemberton had a busy evening stitching up the wounds of several players including Martyn Williams who had two wounds to the back of his head.

Carbonneau needed hospital treatment for a broken nose as did Christophe Lamaison while David Venditti was treated for a bite wound to his hand.

Many of the Welsh players headed down to the hotel bar to talk through the evening's events before retiring to their rooms assuming that was the end of the matter.

The following morning the team were due to leave for the flight home and congregated for an 8 a.m. departure. They were shocked to find police outside the hotel. Some of the Brive players had made a complaint and as a consequence of their accusations, Jason and Steele Lewis, Phil John, Andre Barnard and Dale McIntosh were taken in for questioning.

After law enforcement had completed their initial enquiries, everyone was released to fly home apart from

McIntosh, Barnard and John who had to say an extra night to help police with their investigations.

Williams was still receiving letters some six or seven years after the event, as various parties attempted to claim compensation from him as a result of missing work due to injuries received at the bar.

Ponty ended up being fined £30,000, half of that amount being suspended. The punishment was for the on-field fighting and not for the incidents that occurred at the bar.

The two teams met in the return fixture a week later in Pontypridd at Sardis Road, the aforementioned "House of Pain." A pulsating match ended in a 29-29 draw with thankfully very little incident. The Brive players left immediately after the final whistle refusing to stay for any post-match functions.

Carbonneau didn't play in that game, claiming he had suffered serious injuries in the brawl at Bar Toulzac.

If both teams thought that was the end of their brutal exchanges, then they were sadly mistaken. Pontypridd were drawn to face Brive once more in a quarter final play-off back at the Parc Municipal des Sports on 1st November 1997.

Macintosh, John and Barnard had been banned from the region following earlier events so they could not feature. Magistrates would not even allow them in for the day to take part in the match.

Brive won the game 25-20 – yet another close encounter.

Brive visited Toulouse in the semi-final drawing 22-22 but they progressed to the final as a result of outscoring the home side by two tries to one. A month later, on 31st January 1998, Brive lost to Bath 19-18 at Stade du Parc Lescure in Bordeaux in the final where John Callard, the England full back, scored all of Bath's points with a try, a conversion and four penalties.

One of Carbonneau's finer days came at Wembley stadium on 5th April 1998.

92

France went to Wembley, Wales' temporary home, while the Millennium Stadium was under construction. The French were looking to claim their first ever back-to-back Five Nations Grand Slam.

Wales were confident after wins over Scotland and Ireland, but Pierre Villepreux's French side taught them a lesson in forward power and dazzling back play.

Carbonneau and fly-half Thomas Castaignède ran the show. Behind a dominant pack they played dazzling rugby linking up with centre Stéphane Glas time and again to create havoc in the Welsh midfield scoring four first-half tries to give *Les Bleus* a 29-0 half-time lead.

Wales went down to 13 men at one point as Colin Charvis and Stuart Davies were given yellow cards, and France ran in three more tries after the break including one for Fabien Galthié who replaced Carbonneau to seal the double-Slam in style and condemn Wales to their biggest home defeat of all time.

France scored six tries in front of a 72,000 crowd through Sadourny (two) Garbajosa (two) Glas, Thomas Lièvremont and Galthié. Christophe Lamaison, another Brive notable, landed five conversions and two penalties.

The match proved how talented and skillful Carbonneau really was. He had all the scrum- half tricks in his locker, and without all the antagonistic and violent tendencies, he bestrode the Wembley turf with poise, elegance and beauty. His service to Castaignède was immaculate.

Carbonneau's final game for France came in Dublin on 17th February 2001 against Warren Gatland's Ireland in a Six Nations competition that was eventually won by England. The tournament was disrupted by an outbreak of foot and mouth disease and did not actually finish until 20th October of that year, the final match taking place in Dublin where Ireland beat England 20-14 so denying them a Grand Slam.

Carbonneau announced his playing retirement in 2006. He coached at Tarbes, Lannemezan and Brive before stepping away from rugby to concentrate on the clothing brand, Oliphil, which he created with his brother Olivier back in 1998.

The Oliphil stores are fitted out like a rugby pub with red wood paneling, changing rooms, pool tables, beer dispenser. According to the company blurb: "When you enter the shop you are immediately immersed in a chic and sporty universe around the oval ball. Like our products, our stores breathe rugby spirit while remaining elegant." Thank goodness the shop fittings weren't modelled on Bar Toulzac after the mêlée!

The Carbonneaus have 31 stores from Paris in the North to Anglet in the south-west.

Mild-mannered, charming and softly spoken, the off-field Philippe Carbonneau is a world away from the one that donned the number nine jersey for club and country.

Chapter 10

Franck Mesnel
"To err is human, to loaf is Parisian."
Victor Hugo

Pink bow ties, champagne at half-time and a bar crawl on scooters prior to kick-off. These were not the actions of effervescent rugby supporters or elements in an elaborate hospitality package but rather the pre-match preparation for certain members of a French team about to play their biggest game of the season, and for some, their lives. It was a match to determine the winners of the French Rugby Championship.

Franck Mesnel is geographically the most northerly member of my Hard Man XV, hailing from Neuilly-Sur-Seine, one of the most affluent and prestigious residential areas in the whole of France. It is situated some nine kilometers west of Paris in the Hauts-de-Seine department.

Former French President Nicolas Sarkozy along with Edith Piaf and the Duke and Duchess of Windsor lived there while American actress Bette Davis and Greek shipping tycoon Aristotle Onassis spent their final days in the local American hospital. Of these, I suspect it would only have been Edith who could say "Je ne regrette rien" with any conviction.

In the early morning summer sunshine in Neilly-Sur-Seine, Café du Marche is just waking up and following its regular routine. The backboard menus are getting their first taste of chalk while I am getting my much needed first taste of coffee. But today is no ordinary day. This evening 14 miles up the road, one of the most wonderful annual rugby occasions will take place.

A Top 14 Final is a rugby and cultural event like no other. It is Mardi Gras and Oktoberfest all rolled into one.

From early morning the TGVs roll into Gare de Lyon and Gare Montparnasse with their colourful human cargo disembarking and immediately heading for a station espresso with the speed and footwork of Serge Blanco.

The day of the final is an extremely long one with kick off at 9 p.m. Wherever you go in the French capital on that particular June Saturday, there are lines of families in team shirts sitting out in geometric lines of tables as far as the eye can see soaking up the sun's rays amid the wafting aroma of steak frites.

The glass carafes of red, white and rosé glisten in the sun. This is as much a part of final day as the match itself, and just as grueling, with cheese and coffee and, maybe even a brandy to get through before setting off for Stade de France with a heavy stomach and a much lighter wallet.

If you have never been to Paris for the final, I would recommend you add it to your bucket list.

It's not just the fans who add the colour and joie de vivre to the French rugby season's climax. The finals of 1987 and 1990 were memorable for more than just the rugby thanks to Racing 92, the Parisian outfit, and their famous fly-half Franck Mesnel who is my selection to wear the number 10 shirt in this exclusive French XV.

Franck agonized over choice of career and had to make a difficult decision to become either a pilot or an architect. He eventually decided on the latter.

Mesnel was the ringleader of a group of eccentric Racing players who got together when they decided to mock their own image as capital city fancy dans who were known collectively as Le Show-Bizz.

"We always kept our values of respect and rugby values, but we had that impertinence" says Mesnel.

Le Show-Bizz painted their boots gold, wore fake bald heads, ran out in blazers and blackened their faces.

"These acts were a motivation for us, and each time we did one of these jokes we knew we had to back it up."

Racing lost to Toulon 15-12 in the 1987 French Championship final. They wore pink bow ties for the first time but three years later they went to another level when they faced a hard-nosed down-to-earth and tough Agen team in the season finale at Parc des Princes.

Racing won 22-12 after extra time but the match is best remembered for the incredible sight of Mesnel and his Le Show-Bizz colleagues quaffing champagne on the pitch during the half-time team talk.

"One of our wingers who was injured told us he would come on at half-time with the champagne" says Mesnel. "It was real champagne on a silver salver. I just remember seeing the faces of Pierre Berbizier and the Agen team looking at us in amazement, but it did us good since we won the second half."

President François Mitterrand left that final with a gift from French international Jean Baptiste Lafond in the form of a pink bow tie which the full back presented to him before kick-off.

Le Show-Bizz became such a phenomenon and attracted so much attention that Franck Mesnel, Eric Blanc and Lafond released a record, a single entitled "Quand tu marques un essai" ("When you score a try.")

Former Welsh fly-half Jonathan Davies recalls some great battles against Mesnel. "Firstly, Franck was a lovely bloke, but he was a big lump, he ran hard and straight and was a handful to tackle. He changed the way French fly-halves played. He took the ball up to line and looked for contact, unlike the jinking fleet-footed number tens France were used to. He was a ferocious tackler, hard but never dirty."

France, a bit like Wales, had always looked on the fly-half as the play maker, the jinky side- stepping diminutive figure who ran the show. Guy Camberabero, the number 10 in France's 1968 Grand Slam-winning side, was all of 5ft 7 in and weighed in at just over 10 stones.

Grand Slam-winning fly-half of the Seventies Jean-Pierre Romeu, the brilliant kicker from Montferrand, was an unusual sight at the time as he was 6ft tall, an anomaly for a fly-half, but even then he still only weighed in at 11st 7lbs. Slight as he might have been, there were aspects of his play that made it logical that his adopted Montferrand had once been a crusader fortress.

Franck Mesnel tipped the scales at 14st 5lbs and was just under six feet tall. He was the pathfinder for the big number tens that were to follow.

Mesnel constantly broke the gain line with his upper body strength and muscular thighs, and with Phillipe Sella outside him, opposition defences must have felt that they were caught between the devil and the deep *Les Bleus* sea.

World Rugby CEO Brett Gosper was playing for Racing when Mesnel arrived at the club.

"Franck was playing in a third division Parisian suburb club, Saint-Germain. His mate was a scrum-half in Racing's second team, and it was he who told our coach that he had a friend who was a very good player and who he would bring along to training.

"We were playing touch rugby and Franck really looked good, his hands, the way he sidestepped. We thought he probably couldn't tackle, but boy *could* he tackle.

"I had the pleasure of playing four seasons right next to Franck at the Racing Club from 1986 when he arrived to 1989 when I left. With Racing, he was mostly calling the shots at fly-half and I was at centre, usually pairing with his soon to be brother-in-law, Éric Blanc. He was gifted with everything a normal rugby player could only dream of. Thighs that were the envy of our props but possessing great speed and balance with the ability to step off both feet (rare then) and a right boot that could send the ball jaw-dropping distances kicking for touch, dropping a goal or converting a try.

"Franck, an introverted, even nervous, picture of politeness and hesitation in a bar or night club was the master of timing and serenity on the field. Unflappable and unmovable, he could calmly assess any situation and deploy any of his many skills to get Racing out of trouble or put the opposition in serious trouble.

"His heavy frame was in complete contradiction with the lightness of touch with which he went about dominating a game. Occasionally though, the big unit was launched directly into enemy lines with devastating effect in attack or defence. Franck could also calm a back line with his sense of humour, not something you would expect from a normally tormented French fly-half. His habit of pointing out the comical on the field was a display of calm and confidence that spread through the rest of the team and drove the very special showman-like attitude of the great Racing Club team of that era."

The Racing coach at the time was legendary hard man and prop Robert Paparemborde.

Franck Mesnel remembers: "I met 'Papa' and I lied to him by telling him I was a fly-half when in fact I was a centre at Saint-Germain. I had pace but Robert soon realized I wasn't a fly-half because of my kicking."

Paparemborde signed Mesnel and within a year of his move to Racing, he was playing in the first ever Rugby World Cup against the All Blacks at Eden Park.

In 1986 he made his international debut for *Les Bleus* in "The Battle of Nantes", the match between France and New Zealand that also marked the debut of Pascal Ondarts.

"I grew up in Carrières-sur-Seine and my friend used to take me to his home to watch the Five Nations on television. I was a huge fan of the Wales team so to play in the Five Nations in 1987 was a dream come true.

"Playing at Twickenham for the first time during the 1987 Five Nations championship was my fourth appearance for France. I'd started rugby quite late at the age

99

of 25 after finishing my studies to qualify as an architect. I wanted to play at the home of rugby at least once and after that everything was a bonus."

The bonus for him was that he scored a drop goal in that match and that France went on to complete a clean sweep and win a Grand Slam.

Franck played in the 1987 Rugby World Cup final, and after returning from New Zealand he founded the fashion company Eden Park, named after the venue of the final. The company emblem is the now world-famous pink bow tie.

The Eden Park company became a global success, and in 2016 the company declared a turnover of €60m.

Mesnel went on to play 56 times for France, 32 at centre, and 24 at fly-half. He scored eight tries and three drop goals. His final appearance for France was on 22nd June 1995 in the Rugby World Cup third place play-off against England in South Africa. The match ended in a victory for *Les Bleus*, a perfect way to head into the international rugby sunset along with Phillipe Sella who also played his last game that day.

Franck Mesnel, like Jean-Pierre Rives, was a man who took his humour and fun very seriously and with a constant regard for the game's traditions, values and ethos.

Le Show-Bizz antics are now enshrined in French rugby folklore but many of the stunts would not be readily accepted in today's politically correct society.

On 11th January 1987 when Racing took on Bayonne in the heart of the Basque country, the players ran out onto the field wearing the region's traditional Basque berets in honour of the great full-backs of the past who hailed from Bayonne.

In the French Championship quarter-finals on 19th April 1987 when Racing faced Brive at Clermont-Ferrand, the Racing players, led by Franck, ran out of the changing rooms wearing blazers and bowties. The following week, at the semi-final in Bordeaux, Le Show-Bizz left behind their traditional rugby shorts and instead faced a strong Toulouse outfit wearing Harem pants.

The Eden Park Four of Éric Blanc, Yvon Rosset, Jean-Baptiste Lafond plus Philippe Guillard and Mesnel hit upon the bowtie during a dinner when they were trying to think of a fitting accessory to represent the spirit of their team. The colour pink was already a club trademark and the team mascot was the Pink Panther. During a key match against Toulouse on 10th April 1988, the Racing squad painted their faces and limbs with black make-up to celebrate the birthday of Racing's African player, Vincent "Momo" Lelano.

In February 1989 during a match against Béziers, Jean Baptiste Lafond played the entire match wearing a false bald head, in friendly mockery of his opponent Didier Camberabero who had recently been fitted with a hairpiece.

When playing a match at their home ground of Stade Colombes, all the backs in the squad decided to celebrate the bicentenary of the French Revolution in their own way. In a match against Le Boucau, they arrived on the pitch wearing long striped shorts in the revolutionary colours of blue, white and red, and sporting Phrygian caps, the headgear that symbolizes the French Revolution.

The year following their champagne-quaffing final against Agen, Racing were knocked out in the semi-finals. But Mesnel and company showed they hadn't lost their sense of humour; when facing Béziers for the third-place play-off, they arrived at Stade Jean-Bouin on bikes and wearing berets. They entered the stadium and cycled two laps around the athletics track saluting spectators.

Throughout those years, Le Show-Bizz players consistently attached great importance to French elegance. Even on the field, they turned up their collars, always kept their socks pulled up high and sometimes lengthened their shorts. They looked after their shoes and jazzed them up with white laces. This attitude was part and parcel of the stringent standards they insisted on upholding, both in sport and in their appearance.

Mesnel is quick to point out: "These acts were a motivation for us. Each time we did one of these jokes we knew we had to back it up on the field."

Many French sportsmen and women refer to retirement as "la petite mort", the little death. Of course, there is a sexual meaning as well but people in all sports reach for phrases of this kind to express the melancholy that can follow retirement. Franck Mesnel on the other hand experienced a rebirth.

His high-end fashion label Eden Park saved him from the vacuum that can consume any athlete when their sporting days come to a close.

A career from architect to rugby player to the founder of a chic fashion establishment is a path that has not been trodden by too many fly-halves. Just for good measure, Mesnel also used to be in a boy band in the early Eighties.

"I'm from a generation that moved its backside" says Mesnel. "As a family we had enough to eat but were not well off. You had to look after your money."

"I have to be under pressure. I am built like that – sport and business give me that feeling."

It is this work ethic and mental strength that made him such a tough opponent. He would never stop battling or give in on the rugby pitch or in the boardroom.

He says: "There are many similarities between rugby and business. You need to be highly motivated in both."

Now I must confess that I am no fashion guru, and as a man who spends more time in Primark than Eden Park, the prospect of spending £45 on a pair of pants fills me with horror. The company does however sell two pairs of trainer socks at the bargain price of £39, prices harder to tackle than a rampaging Mesnel in his rugby prime.

In 2005 as he began to hit middle age, he took up flying. Planes gave way to helicopters in 2011. Mesnel says: "I was always on team projects. As I approached my fifties, I wanted to do something alone, something for myself."

A lovely touch came in 2010 when he bought the rugby posts at the Eden Park ground in Auckland to raise money for the Christchurch earthquake appeal. One of the posts was cut into shapes and made into trophies which were presented to the All Blacks team that won the 1987 Rugby World Cup.

Now a multi-millionaire, Mesnel has a busy life that doesn't leave him an awful lot of time for rugby, and like many of the rugby players of his era, he finds that the modern attritional professional game leaves a lot to be desired.

"Sometimes it is a bit boring, you now have 30 supermen on the field all trying to the break the door down."

Chapter 11

Yoann Huget
"The French are predictably unpredictable."
Andrew Mehrtens

The trite question that was regurgitated to the point of annoyance and trotted out before almost every French international match: "Which France team will turn up?" has died a death in recent years due to the slump in the fortunes of the national side.

This was down to the fact that it finally got to the stage where, rather sadly, we all knew exactly which French team would turn up.

However, in the case of Yoann Huget that maxim still rings true. It is fair to say that you never know which version of the winger will turn up, if indeed he manages to turn up at all.

If any player exhibited genius, brutality and bewildering comedic error in equal measure, often in the same phase of play, then it is my left-wing selection.

This was a strong lethal finisher who could lose his cool and his concentration in an instant, going from a match-winner with blistering pace and lethal footwork to the source of catastrophic errors that could, and sometimes did, cost his team dearly.

Selecting the wingers for my French Hard Men XV took a lot of thought. One winger who deserved selection purely down to the dreadful bad luck he suffered was Gaston Vareilles whose international career was ruined by a baguette.

In 1911 France beat Scotland in Paris to record their first ever win in the Five Nations Championship.

The fact that France won 16-15 is overshadowed by the tragic tale of a young Frenchman selected to play on the wing that day. He was no doubt overflowing with a mixture of nerves and excitement as he headed northwards by train through beautiful French countryside on a day he would never forget, for all the wrong reasons.

Gaston Vareilles was a wing at Stade Français. When the train stopped at Lyon, Gaston nipped out of his carriage to visit the station buffet for a baguette. By the time he had been served, he returned to the platform to see his train chugging off into the distance.

Back in Paris, one of the spectators, French sprinter André Francquenelle, volunteered to make up the numbers and he did rather well. In fact he went on to earn another two French caps.

Poor old Gaston did eventually make it to the stadium in time for the kick-off, but was told in no uncertain terms where to go.

He never played for France again and ended up working as a planter in French Indochina, before his death on 15th January 1929.

However Gaston also holds a more uplifting statistic to his name, he scored France's first ever drop goal against Wales in Cardiff in 1908, a slice of good fortune as the home crowd sang "Bread of Heaven", but sadly it is that station baguette that he will be always be remembered for.

Pamiers is a commune in the Occitanie region of south-west France where the mountains are responsible for cold nights, in contrast with the warm days, a factor that gives the local wines a concentrated taste. Monks of the Saint Antonin de Fredelas abbey made wine here in the Middle Ages that was transported to Bordeaux and across the Channel to England. The town is the birthplace of two notable sons, composer Gabriel Fauré and my chosen recipient of the Hard Men number 11 shirt, French international Yoann Huget.

Yoann Huget's career has had more ups and downs than a runaway roller coaster or the Italians' currency when they had the lira. In 2015 he was given a formal warning for feigning injury during Toulouse's European Champions Cup defeat to Bath. He made an extravagant theatrical dive in an attempt to gain a penalty, not his finest hour, and one of a catalogue of indiscretions in a career that has certainly not been dull.

More histrionics followed in the Six Nations match between France and Italy in Paris.

Huget reacted quickest to his chip-and-chase into the Italian "22" and Bellini was forced to turn before racing back. Bellini was level with Huget as they both homed in on the bounce. As Huget crossed in front and nudged the ball into the in-goal area, Bellini instinctively grabbed at Huget's waist momentarily and quickly released. But Huget being Huget, threw his hands in the air and recoiled dramatically rather than following the ball. Bellini touched the ball down in goal while Huget rolled around claiming a penalty try.

Huget had been impeded, albeit for a split second, so after referring to the TMO, referee Matt Carley had no option but to award a penalty try and to yellow-card Bellini, another example of Huget's unsavoury side.

In 2015, in a Top 14 clash between Bordeaux and Toulouse, Huget was making his way to the Bordeaux try line when he lashed out with his right foot into the face of Andre Marais, who was prone on the ground. Huget's studs smashed into his opponent's face and the sickening television footage caused global outrage in rugby circles. To compound matters, the Toulouse wing was not red-carded, yellow-carded, or even sanctioned post-match.

Clermont's Canadian international Jamie Cudmore labelled Huget a coward, saying: "Run of play is one thing but intentionally stepping on someone's face is another level."

Another item on the charge sheet involved a three-month ban for breaking doping regulations in 2011 and it was swiftly followed by a further ban for having missed three doping controls. As a result of these, Huget missed the 2011 Rugby World Cup tournament.

Yoann Huget seems to have lived a somewhat charmed life with regard to biting; the tooth marks seen in George North's arm during the 2017 France vs Wales match in Paris could not be attributed to any particular French player due to lack of footage available from the host broadcaster, despite referee Wayne Barnes' referral to the TMO. I have studied the subsequent video footage on many occasions since, and all I can say is Monsieur Huget was in the close vicinity.

To add insult to (literal) injury, France coach Guy Novès, suggested in the post-match press conference that North may well have bitten himself, an allegation that must have confounded the many surgeons and doctors who play the game and sent them scurrying to restudy *Gray's Anatomy*.

Another match against Wales in 2019 saw one of Huget's classic aberrations. Having attempted to dive on the ball as it crossed his own dead ball line, with no opposition player in sight, the ball slipped from his grasp and George North raced in from distance to touch down for a crucial Welsh try that turned the course of the game and propelled Wales to an eventual Grand Slam.

"Thanks to my sloppiness, I let doubt creep in to the team. We were in front at the time but my mistake killed the mood" recalls Huget.

Wales centre Hadleigh Parkes says: "I shinned the kick – it was a shocker but all credit to George [North], he kept chasing and luckily the bounce went our way. I did feel sorry for Huget."

In the following match of the tournament at Twickenham. Huget's Jekyll and Hyde syndrome revealed itself once again.

Selected at full back, he had a torrid time running the ball back from deep and being constantly flattened by the Vunipola brothers.

He dropped high balls, was caught out of position and was substituted at half-time but not before he made a glorious searing break down the right to set up a try for Damian Penaud.

France lost 44-8 to England. They conceded a try 66 seconds after kick-off and were 30-8 down at half-time. As implosions go, even by French standards, this was spectacular.

Huget said: "Playing at wing feels more natural to me. The defensive aspect is a little different at full-back."

That match was a humiliation for a French side that already had a humiliation loyalty card.

The press agreed with Huget's assessment and the following day gave him a 4/10 in their player ratings. It read as follows:

Yoann Huget: "A remarkable performance, bright in attack but showed utter disdain for defensive duties and was hooked at half time. One day England's opponents will pick a full- back at 15."

That defeat proved to be a watershed moment for France.

The French rugby paper *Midi Olympique* carried the front-page headline "WATERLOO!" I assume it was referring to the battle and not the station, but either way France had gone totally off the rails. The journalist might have been thinking of the French ambassador who, on being shown the revamped Waterloo station in 1922, said: "C'est magnifique, mais ce n'est pas la gare?"

England kicked mercilessly behind the French defence that day, and France's back three, rather than adjusting and dropping deeper, stood transfixed while leaving acres of space behind them for England to exploit.

After that match, coach Jacques Brunel (no relation to railway and station engineer Isambard Kingdom) was on borrowed time. It was too close to the 2019 Rugby World Cup for a regime change but Fabien Galthie was brought in to assist. A number of players from France's Under 21 World Cup-winning squad were introduced, and a new dawn was ushered in producing a French rugby sunrise when Galthie took over as head coach after the Rugby World Cup.

Yoann Huget did however have some happy days when facing England, particularly in 2004 when *Les Bleus* beat *Les Rosbifs* 26-24 in Paris.

Huget scored after just 30 seconds from a Jules Plisson grubber kick to record one of the fastest tries in Six Nations history though not quite as fast as that of Scot John Leslie's try only 10 seconds after kick-off at Murrayfield in the 1999 Five Nations match against Wales.

I hear you ask: "So why on earth choose Huget?" Well so far, I have discussed his minuses in great detail; they were frequent and plentiful. But Yoann was big, fast and elusive as a dog at a fair. He could also dazzle you with the sheer beauty of his rugby. He was, on his day, a deadly finisher and a runner who could scorch the turf. So, despite all the negatives, he was one of the best attacking wings in the world game.

At 6ft 2in and 15st 12lb, it is only when you see him up close that you realize what a physical specimen he truly is. His size and power are not always visible from high up in the stands but at pitch level you really get an appreciation of the power and strength, attributes that make him such a deadly finisher.

He has been on the end of many a glorious French move, culminating with his trademark military salute after each touchdown.

His club career began at Toulouse back in 2005 before returning to the Pink City in 2012 after stints with Agen and Bayonne.

Huget is a Catholic who often prays before matches. His grandfather's influence had a great impact on his religious faith. The tattoo on his left side (his wife has an identical one) reads (in French) "Only God can judge." His faith has been a great comfort during difficult times in his career.

His international debut came at Stade de Mosson in Montpellier on 20th November 2010 where he joined a back line with Rougerie, Jauzion and Andreu with Damien Traille in the unusual role of fly-half. France beat the Pumas 15-9. Fellow Hard Men XV selections Sebastien Chabal, the aforementioned Rougerie and Guilhem Guirado, were also in France's squad that day.

In 2013 he married French actress Fanny Veyrac who is best known for the film *Paris monopole* in which, you've guessed it, the Paris equivalent of the board game "Monopoly" features. The arrival of their daughter Myla in 2015 gave Yoann a different perspective on life; he must have felt that Community Chest in the "Monopoly" cards had been especially generous.

Having spent 11 years with Stade Toulousain, albeit in two stints, Huget and the club and indeed the city of Toulouse, have inseparable bonds.

The bearded winger has been an integral part of the club's revival in recent years, while playing a thrilling and entertaining brand of rugby that has been appreciated by the entire rugby fraternity.

Huget rounded off a brilliant 2018/19 season by scoring two tries against Clermont in the dream Top 14 final at Stade de France, in front of a packed 79,000 crowd. Toulouse were victorious 24-18 victory on a warm, sultry Parisian June night.

The winger's form earned him a place in France's 2019 Rugby World Cup squad.

After scoring a try in *Les Bleus'* 33-9 win over the USA in Fukuoka, he was in the side to face Wales at the quarter final stages where France suffered an agonizing last-minute defeat.

France started 2020 with new blood and a new spring in their step. It appears that Yoann Huget's international career ended in the Land of the Rising Scrum. But, the Toulouse wing has been written off so many times that you would never bet against a recall, although, as is the case with us all, age may just be catching up with him.

As this written chapter draws to a close, Yoann Huget's rugby chapter rolls on, very much like the Garonne river that flows through his beloved Toulouse, cascading down to the Gironde estuary before finally reaching the Atlantic.

In October 2017, he signed a contract extension with Stade Toulousain taking him through to his retirement in 2021.

Huget may have been all at sea on many occasions during his rugby career, but I prefer to remember those glorious moments when he was riding the crest of a wave.

Chapter 12

Mathieu Bastareaud
"Other countries drink to get drunk, and this is accepted by everyone. In France drunkenness is a consequence and never an intention."
Roland Barthes

Winston Churchill once described Russia as being a riddle, wrapped in a mystery, inside an enigma. It's a phrase that could certainly be used of Mathieu Bastareaud.

His parents hailed from Guadalupe, an archipelago in the Caribbean, which is in fact an overseas region of France with the Euro as its official currency. French, Antillean and Creole are the official languages.

Mathieu's parents divorced when he was only three years old and from then on he lived with his mother, Dania.

Some 5,927 miles east from Guadalupe lies Massy where the family moved. It is a suburb of Paris located ten miles south of the Eiffel tower, an area crowded with nondescript residential tower blocks, one of a plethora of "banlieues" that stretch out for mile after mile. It's a face of Paris that visitors rarely see except for the odd glimpse while traveling past on an RER train.

There were not many escape routes from the grim reality of this poverty stricken and crime ridden area of Paris, but fortunately for Mathieu, he found one in the form of sport.

Coach Jean-Max Calice brought a young Mathieu to Massy Rugby Club and remembers vividly the first time he saw him play.

"He was playing at a junior tournament, he was absolutely incredible. Even at the tender age of 13 he was extremely strong but what struck me most of all was his will to win. I've never coached a greater competitor."

"Mathieu became a symbol for the banlieues, a symbol of hope. He's a great role model, very humble and respectful, and has a lovely sense of humour. Family and friends are very important to him."

For those rugby fans who have only witnessed the rugby persona of the big centre, they may find it surprising to discover that Bastareaud remains one of rugby's most misunderstood and complicated characters.

"I've always been afraid of failure and judgement, whether it be rugby or school exams" he says. "I don't like to disappoint people – knowing that I'm going to be judged makes me doubt my ability."

The question of validation may come from a complicated relationship with his father, which is well documented.

It was Bastareaud père who encouraged him to take up rugby but when Mathieu received his first international call-up to the France U19 set-up, the glorious moment was soured by his father's reaction.

Excited and elated by the news of his international debut and wanting to share the good news, he woke his dad up from a nap to relay the news. His father's reply was: "Okay, is that all?" That would dampen a damp-proof squib. We can all be amateur psychologists at times, but you don't need to be Sigmund Freud or Carl Jung to appreciate the effect this had on the young Bastareaud.

He moved from Massy to join Parisian city-slickers Stade Français in 2007 and made 99 appearances for the boys in pink.

In 2001, Toulon President, Mourad Boudjellal showed an interest in bringing Bastareaud to the Stade Mayol. He said "Mathieu Bastareaud is suffering from a form of depression and is no longer psychologically able to play for Stade Français."

Stade were adamant that Bastareaud would see out the remaining two years of his contract, and this kicked off a tug of love between the two clubs for the big man's services.

The one and only Bernard Laporte, Stade's president at the time, got involved, as he does with most things, and announced that "Bastareaud is a child of Stade Français and I have spoken to the player and he is happy to stay."

Eventually, as is the way in French rugby, it was money that did the talking, and a big transfer fee from Toulon persuaded a financially unstable Stade club to part with their number one crowd pleaser.

Way back in 1888, Vincent van Gogh left a dull grey Paris and headed south by train for the unique almost heavenly light of Provence.

"May artists come together in Provence" was van Gogh's wish.

Bastareaud, like van Gogh, headed south to join the rugby artists that included Matt Giteau, whose delicate brush strokes were complemented by a big man with the rugby equivalent of a roller and two litres of emulsion.

In July 2011 he signed a three-year contract with Toulon and in fact stayed in the south of France for eight years being made club captain for the 2017/18 season.

His mental problems raised their ugly head once again in 2014 after his club Toulon lost 30-6 to Stade Français. He broke down in tears and gave an emotional interview saying: "You have to know how to face up to things. I haven't been able to find my form. I'm a zombie. I think that I've now come to the end of the road. There comes a time when you have to say stop."

The self-doubt that fills this big man is a world away from his on-field persona of a confident, rampaging beast of a rugby player, and it has frequently blighted his career. He has also struggled constantly to overcome prejudice in its many forms, the quest to find an inner peace and tranquility to match the bone-jarring tackling and arm-wrenching breakdown work has been an elusive one.

A checkered disciplinary record includes a suspension for making homophobic remarks to Benetton's Italian international Sebastian Negri at the Stade Mayol.

Also, in a Top 14 match between Toulon and Castres, he took exception to being obstructed and took revenge on Christophe Samson. Samson and Delilah this wasn't though somebody's head was indeed almost on a platter!

As Samson was slowing down the ball at a ruck, by not releasing the ball on the floor, Bastareaud launched himself to clear out the player and then went back for a second attempt with a forearm smash to the face. He received a red card and a lengthy ban.

But his pièce de résistance took place in Wellington during France's tour to New Zealand in 2009 when he lied about an assault that he alleged had taken place after France lost 14-10 to the All Blacks.

Bastareaud claimed he had been assaulted by a group of men at a taxi rank while returning to the team hotel. He appeared with severe facial injuries supposedly caused by the attack but this turned out to be utter fabrication by the French centre.

The story resulted in New Zealand Prime Minister, John Key, issuing an apology on behalf of the nation and he launched a police investigation into the "attack."

Bastareaud decided to come clean, much to the embarrassment of the French Rugby Federation, when he revealed the injuries were actually caused when he fell in his hotel room while drunk.

He explained: "I lost my balance when getting undressed. I fell awkwardly and smashed a little table. I ended up bleeding a lot and my cheekbone was a real mess and I panicked."

The French Rugby Federation ordered him to complete community service and he was suspended for three months but the consequences of his charade turned out be more severe than he could imagine.

When Mathieu returned home to France, the aftermath of the New Zealand incident resulted in a tough time for him and his family.

"Journalists would try to go to my mother's house and they telephoned my father. It was very hard for them" he says.

On top of all that, Basta found all the online abuse regarding his actions in New Zealand too much, and one day he simply snapped.

"I jumped up from my computer and walked into the kitchen. I took a big knife and slit my veins, immediately collapsing to the floor."

His friends, who were in the living room, heard the noise and ran into the kitchen to discover Bastareaud unconscious on the floor in a large pool of blood together with a knife.

"I don't know if I really wanted to die, I wanted to punish myself" he says. "I kept reading everywhere what a loser I was and it got to me big-time."

He was rushed to hospital and treated but the physical and mental wounds took quite some time to heal.

A troubled childhood during which he suffered from bulimia and depression, led in later life to a battle with alcoholism. Bastareaud was a troubled soul there is no doubt.

His sports psychologist Meriem Salmi says: "Athletes are always on the verge of breaking up. In Mathieu Bastareaud's case, no one would have thought that he could be affected by depression. He's still a colossus with exceptional capabilities and a head. Until the last moment, until the day he attempted suicide he was in training."

"With everything that happened in New Zealand where the whole world was talking about him, he ended up falling apart when the media went to his parents' house."

His family becoming involved was the final straw.

Bastareaud did not feature in the 2009 November international series. France coach Marc Lièvremont wanted the big centre to improve his fitness by training more consistently. "It has been over a year now that we are trying to make him understand that he doesn't do enough to be competitive at a major tournament like the Rugby World Cup" said Lièvremont.

It's a good job Bastareaud was not around in the early 1930s when Jean 'Le Sultan' Sebedio was in charge of training at the Lézignan club.

A Basque from Saint-Jean-de-Luz, he had a fitness regime with a difference. He used to sit in the middle of the pitch wearing a big sombrero and brandishing a long whip that he would crack to make his players run in circles around him.

Sebedio was a bit of a character. He kept a skeleton in the referee's changing room with a whistle in its jaws to intimidate visiting referees.

I'm not sure how Bastareaud would have would have survived under Sebedio.

An international recall came in time for the 2010 Six Nations, where he scored two tries in France's opening 9-18 victory against Scotland at Murrayfield. France went on to complete a Grand Slam that year and Basta played in every game.

My selection of Mathieu in one of the centre positions may surprise some people. For a big brute of a man, his subtle handling skills often went unnoticed. The distraction of massive hits and bouts of violence overshadowed the delicate touches that he possessed. His ability on the floor was incredible and comparable to that of a top-class back row forward.

His international debut came at the Stade de France against Wales in 2009, the first ever Friday-night Six Nations match, partnering Yannick Jauzion at centre. Jauzion was 6ft 4in and weighed 16st 10lb so there was quite some tonnage in that centre partnership.

117

Mathieu helped to end Wales' hopes of a back-to-back Grand Slam that night with a 21-16 victory.

"I was very nervous before facing Wales. I wasn't even in the original squad but an injury to Maxime Mermoz meant I got the call. My club coach phoned me to say I was in. I thought he was joking and I assumed I would just be on the bench so it was a huge shock when France coach Marc Lièvremont told me I was in the starting fifteen."

A few weeks later in Dublin we saw the perfect example of Basta's rugby version of Beauty and the Beast, as he fended off the great Brian O'Driscoll, swatting him away with his massive paw, before giving a sublime one-handed offload to full-back Clément Poitrenaud.

Despite success and fame, he was constantly engaged in a battle to validate his existence. Sports psychologist Meriem Salmi was brought in to steer the big centre through the choppy waters of his validation issues.

An injury to Guilhem Guirado resulted in Bastareaud being made captain for the match against Wales in Cardiff on 17th March 2018.

"In my first match as captain against Wales I was so nervous I was actually sick before the match. It brought out a lot of emotions, about my problems in New Zealand, and made me think about my parents. My mum was so proud – she supported me through all the good and bad times. It was a very special moment for me and for my family."

Basta captained France on three occasions but all three matches ended in defeats for *Les Bleus*.

The Eternal City of Rome was the scene for his final Test match, on 16th March 2019 where France emerged victorious at Stadio Olimpico by 14-25.

Mathieu announced his international retirement the day after he had been not included in France's squad for the 2019 Rugby World Cup in Japan.

"It has not been an easy road representing my country. My family have been my biggest pride. I'm happy to have made my childhood dream come true."

His playing record for France could not be more symmetrical having played 54 internationals, winning 26, losing 26, and drawing two matches.

He scored five tries for his country, two against Italy and Scotland and one against South Africa.

Many rugby folk will be unaware of Mathieu's wonderful sense of humour. His demeanor on the field of play doesn't give an insight into his sense of fun and joviality. This is one of the reasons why he is such a popular teammate wherever he has played the game. It was only when he was selected for the Barbarians squad in 2019 that his sense of fun and mischief became widely known as he struck up an unusual comedy double act with Baa Baas coach Eddie Jones. Their antics appeared on social media and the world saw a different side to the big man.

Later that year he left his beloved Toulon and signed for Rugby United New York for a reported figure of $45,000 dollars a season.

"I wanted to sign for the Sharks in South Africa, but there was nothing concrete forthcoming, and with a new baby, I decided I needed to be somewhere, safe so New York was the best compromise."

He started off playing in his usual position of centre but it appeared that Basta had piled on the pounds since leaving the south of France and as a result he was soon switched to number eight.

In March 2020, the USA rugby season was cancelled due to the Covid-19 virus outbreak, and Basta signed terms with Lyon in the French Top 14 for two seasons commencing 2020/21.

His final match in the States came against San Diego Legion, the club of his ex-Toulon centre partner Ma'a Nonu.

There were rumours of fall-outs with coaches at San Diego but ultimately Covid called the shots. The big man however had no regrets.

"For me it was important to play in another country. We French are not prone to learning other cultures. I had won everything playing 12 seasons in France. I wanted a new challenge."

Due to the Corona pandemic, Bastareaud was confined to an apartment for over a month with wife and baby but was finally able to return to Toulon where they had to quarantine for a further period.

In 2020 he joined Lyon on a two-year contract where he continued his conversion from centre to number eight.

I will finish this chapter as I started it with a quote from Winston Churchill: "A pessimist sees the difficulty in every opportunity, and an optimist sees the opportunity in every difficulty." This quote was used by Mathieu Bastareaud's psychologist, Meriem Salmi, to illustrate the fact that a depressive episode is an opportunity to take stock, rebalance your life and start back even stronger.

We all hope that in the future Mathieu's opportunities far outweigh his difficulties.

Chapter 13

Philippe Sella
*"Everything ends this way in France – everything
weddings, christenings, duels, burials, swindlings,
diplomatic affairs. Everything is a perfect pretext for a
good dinner."*
Jean Anouilh

The French have an expression, "Puer le rugby", which
literally means to stink of rugby. It's an expression they use
to describe someone born to play the sport.

Former France scrum-half and coach
Jacques Fouroux once said that Phillipe Sella had the
strength of a bull combined with the touch of a piano player.

One of the true greats of the game, Sella had a simple
playing philosophy: "It's all about running across the turf
and passing a ball around with your friends" he says.

Let me start this chapter by apologizing for the fact that
my obsession with the twinning of towns has appeared
again.

The French town of Agen is twinned with Llanelli. This
time, I can't think of a twinning anywhere in the world that
could be more appropriate.

They are two rugby-mad towns that live and breathe the
game, where rugby is the topic in every cafe, supermarché
and boulangerie and yes – believe it or not – there is a
boulangerie in Llanelli!

In Agen before you even reach the town, the service
station on the A62 lets you know that rugby is the name of
the game here. It is a shrine to the local rugby club with
oval ball memorabilia displayed throughout the premises.

Now I was born in Carmarthen and spent my early years
in Kidwelly just seven miles down the road from Stradey
Park, the home of the Scarlets.

Old women on the doorsteps used to talk about Delme, Phil, Grav, J. J. and co.; they knew all about rucking and mauling techniques, line-out ploys and angles of attack. Every day was a rugby education and I know that things are exactly the same in Agen.

It has to be said though, in meteorological terms, the towns are worlds apart. The green green grass of home doesn't get that colour without plenty of the wet stuff.

Phillipe Sella played his club rugby in Agen for 13 years between 1982 and 1995, years where he was feted and adored so much that became known to all and sundry as "Monsieur Agen".

He says that the Lot department is part of his story. "I remember Clairac, a beautiful village with its beach and dam where I often used to swim."

"My whole family were athletic – rugby, cycling, basketball and at the age of nine I joined the local rugby league team. I played for Agen aged 18 and France as a 20-year-old."

A try in the France vs England match at Parc des Princes in 1986 captured the poetic beauty and sheer heart-stopping majesty of Sella in his pomp and could also have provided the definition of French rugby at its most sublime.

A France scrum just outside their own "22", Berbizier puts the ball in, 20 seconds later Phillipe Sella is running behind the England posts and touching down for a try.

In between those two acts, all artistic and sporting forms combine from opera to ballet, from gymnastics to athletics along with sleight of hand and fleetness of foot.

Berbizier passes to fly-half Guy Laporte, a missed pass reaches Charvet who feeds Éric Bonneval ten metres from his own line.

Bonneval makes an arrow-straight run up the centre of the field, a mesmerizing 75 metres gained, interspersed with a swerve and dummy before passing high and left to Denis Charvet 30 metres from the English line.

Charvet takes the high pass, flirting with the touch-line, teasing the England defence before delivering the final pass to Sella to apply the coup de grâce.

As *Les Bleus* run back to the half-way line, the sheer joy that is etched on their faces in the hot Parisian sunshine reflects the brilliance of their artistry as the crowd rises to its feet as one and in homage, witnessing French rugby the way they dream it should be played.

The Basque band beat their drums a little louder as Laporte kicks the conversion.

How we long for these moments, just one scissors move, a dummy, a swerve, a flick of the hips, a swagger or even just the look of unadulterated joy on a player's face. If you play France in Paris with the sun on their backs, then you don't have a chance. That used to be the natural order of things .

A 45-minute drive from Agen lies Tonneins, an unremarkable town in the Lot-et-Garonne department of France. Until the early 2000s it was the tobacco capital of France but now the town that stands above the river Garonne between Marmande and Agen has an agricultural emphasis and produces maize, rapeseed and sunflowers.

An unremarkable town, maybe, but in 1962 it produced one truly remarkable rugby player, Phillipe Sella, the prince of centres.

Phillipe Sella and I were both born on 14th February. Sadly that is where our similarities begin and end. If only I had been granted a scintilla of the rugby magic he possessed then I should have been truly blessed.

He combined athletic beauty and ruthlessness like a compound of Rudolf Nureyev and Attila the Hun.

Blessed with great pace, he had the ability to glide away from tackles. He was also extremely strong for a man of modest proportions; he stood 5ft 10in and weighed 13 stone 3lb. And when you add the fact that he was also outstanding in the air, it all adds up to one pretty impressive rugby playing specimen.

He puts his strength down to hours of physical toil on his parents' farm during his youth. They had 70 acres incorporating grain, potatoes and tobacco plants.

"I didn't need a gym or weights" says Sella. "I was naturally fit and full of energy."

Another trademark of his game was his ferocious tackling. England centre Jerry Guscott described being tackled by Sella as "Like being hit by a telephone box swinging on the end of a crane."

Phillipe Sella practically owned that glorious blue number 13 shirt. Anyone else who has filled it since has had a huge act to follow. The red rooster embroidered on the left breast looked just that little bit smaller on everyone else.

Incidentally, the rooster emblem dates back to ancient history. The Romans laughed at the Gauls because in Latin, the word "Gallus" means Gaul but it also means rooster.

The French kings adopted the rooster as a symbol of courage and bravery, and during the French Revolution it became the symbol of the people and of the state.

Phillipe created more records than Quincy Jones and Phil Spector put together.

A hundred and eleven caps for France, 104 at centre, six on the wing and one at full-back is impressive. He played 45 Test matches in succession and captained France on six occasions. Playing for the national team for 13 consecutive seasons is quite a feat.

A more dubious record is the one he holds for being the only French centre to receive a red card, handed out for punching, in a match against Canada in 1984, the only time France have lost to a North American nation.

Pierre Berbizier, the French coach, said he did not deserve to be sent off after Sella was suspended for one match.

"Sella was only pushing away a Canadian player, and the video only shows him trying to push away an opponent who was trying to put his fingers in his eye."

His French debut came in Bucharest on Sunday 31st October 1982 in a 13-9 defeat to Romania. To add injury to insult, he had to spend the night in hospital with concussion following the match and was only made aware of the defeat when he came to his senses the following morning.

He started with a pudding bowl haircut that proceeded over time to become long flowing locks that matched his hair-raising long flowing runs.

In his 111 appearances for *Les Bleus* he tasted victory on 72 occasions, drawing five times and losing 34 matches. France won six Five Nations titles during his reign including a Grand Slam in 1987 while scoring 125 points which was the cumulative total of 30 tries.

Cap number 100, achieved in June 1994, was particularly memorable as France beat the All blacks 22-8 in Christchurch.

Phillipe's final international appearance came on 22nd June 1995 in Pretoria during the Rugby World Cup third place play-off match in which France beat England 19-9.

Regarded as one of the world's best ever centres, it is sometimes forgotten that Sella played on the wing for his first seven games in the French shirt before switching to the midfield for a glorious career where his centre partners included such luminaries as Didier Codorniou, Denis Charvet, Franck Mesnel and Thierry Lacroix.

Charvet said of Sella: "Phillipe was a locomotive, you just had to follow him."

In 1986 he scored a try in each of France's Five Nations matches, a remarkable feat achieved by only two other Frenchmen, Patrick Estève ("TGV") in 1983 and Philippe Bernat-Salles in 2001.

Phillipe Sella is "Mr Agen." He played for the club for 13 years between 1982 and 1985 before heading across the Channel for a spell with Saracens.

The year 1987 was memorable for Sella and one in which he scored a wonderful try at Twickenham against England in the Five Nations. "We were under pressure from an England attack and I can't explain exactly what happened but I intercepted the ball and 70 metres later I had scored a try. It was great!"

Later that year, France reached the first ever Rugby World Cup final in New Zealand where they faced the tournament hosts.

"Obviously I remember the result, but another memory is pre-match. We were all under the posts with the coach, Jacques Fouroux, one and a half hours before the game. Fouroux was speaking about our friends, our families. It was not like now where you could speak easily with them on your mobiles. They were very far away from us and it was an emotional moment to spend together, a strong moment.

"It was marvelous but maybe our emotion was too much before the match. The All Blacks were very strong, they had scored a lot of points in all the games before. That was the difference, we had already played a number of hard games against Scotland, Fiji and Australia.

"During the first half it was very close and we could have led at half-time, our forwards were strong enough to score, but we didn't, even though we were very near to the line." (New Zealand led 9-0 at the break).

"In the second half it was different. After 10-20 minutes the All Blacks were fresher. We needed to take the initiative like we did."

"In the semi-final we carried the ball more, but the All Blacks were very strong. We had no regrets."

In 1996 Sella moved to English club Saracens and along with fly-half Michael Lynagh, he helped to guide the club through the transition between the amateur and professional eras.

"I wanted to learn English and I had never left Agen before. My life had become a bit too comfortable."

His nickname when in France "Fi Fi" was revealed to his teammates by the great Australian Lynagh who wore the number ten shirt for the north London club. I gather it caused a great deal of amusement among the squad.

At the age of 36, his final rugby match took place at Twickenham in 1998 in the final of the Tetley Bitter Cup between Saracens and Wasps.

Fittingly, he scored Saracens' opening try in which he displayed power, pace and vision in a final gift to the rugby world before leaving its stage. Saracens went on to lift the trophy, defeating Wasps 48-18 in front of a crowd of 65,000.

Many people may not be aware of Phillipe's sense of humour; he is a cheery soul and always up for a laugh.

I caught up with him at Twickenham Stoop when Agen visited Harlequins for a European Challenge Cup match and recollection of one incident brought a smile followed by giggles.

"After a training session with Saracens we went into the Jacuzzi. I took my towel off and went in naked but a few moments later two women got in. I didn't know it was open to the public, I thought it was just for the players. I ended up having to stay in that Jacuzzi for quite some time.

"On another occasion we (France) were playing a tour match in New Zealand. An opposition player attempted a drop-kick which hit the posts and bounced back into play. Serge [Blanco] and I both jumped to catch the ball, missed it and clashed heads with both of us ending up in hospital. To make things worse, the opposition kicker reclaimed the ball and scored a try. We laughed about it in hospital after we had both been stitched up."

127

At the World Rugby Hall of Fame in Warwickshire, into which Sella was inducted in 2008, there is an inscription from the great man himself.

"Rugby – it's a game. It's about meeting people, commitment, involvement, wellbeing, joie de vivre. It is happiness, quite simply.

"This was part of my life and this is still the case today, even if I am no longer involved in the game on a daily basis.

"The word 'rugby' and all that it means and implies is still in my blood."

Phillipe set up "Les Enfants de l'Ovale" which creates educational and sports projects using the skills and values of rugby. "It is about sharing the richness of rugby with children who are not fortunate enough to have a general and sporting education."

Hard but fair, Sella had the odd "moment" such as punching Wallaby forward Peter Fitzsimons. Similarly, England fly-half Rob Andrew was also in receipt of a retaliatory slap from the number 13 in blue.

Sella has played against some of the best centres in the business but does not put anyone in particular at the top of the pile. There is of course a group he rates highly. He admires Welshmen John Devereux and Scott Gibbs along with Wallabies Tim Horan and Jason Little and he also found England's Will Carling a particularly formidable opponent.

Despite his fame, Sella says he did not court adulation or praise. "I was no star, being in the limelight is not my style. I just want to give what I have to offer."

He says his greatest rugby moments came in 1982 when Agen beat Bayonne 18-9 at Parc des Princes to win the French Championship. Sella scored a try after five minutes, the first of four by Agen. Another highlight came in 1987 in the Rugby World Cup semi- final when France beat Australia.

That Rugby World Cup semi-final is regarded as one of the greatest matches of all time. Here is Sella describing that famous try right at the death, a try created not by the silky backs but by the French rugby hard men.

"It couldn't have been much closer. With 80 minutes on the clock, the scores were level at 24-24. Then came Serge Blanco's try. The try was strange because our forwards were playing like backs, everyone seemed to want to join in including the referee who missed a forward pass. Serge's try started with a kick to the middle of the pitch, our lock Alain Lorieux arrived at the ball and caught it. From there the first players up in support were our two props Pascal Ondarts and Jean-Pierre Garuet. They passed the ball between each other like a couple of backs.

The ball went towards the left touchline and Denis Charvet's pass to Éric Champ was forward but the officials didn't see it. Laurent Rodriguez, number eight, picked the ball up off his toes and just about managed to get it to our wing Patrice Lagisquet who gave the final pass to Blanco. He took the ball at full speed and went over in the corner diving at full stretch, it was unbelievable."

In that match Phillipe produced France's opening try, a classic Sella score.

"I can only clearly recall touching the ball down under the posts. Pierre Berbezier gave it to Franck Mesnel who passed to me. I took a gap between two Australians before side-stepping then going over for the try. I looked behind me and there were three Wallabies lying on the ground. A great feeling!"

When anyone sits down to compile their greatest ever rugby XV, there aren't many positions that are cut and dried. Most can be hotly debated well into the early hours but there are a couple of exceptions.

While writing the numbers from 1-15 on the left-hand side of the page, there are two numbers that pretty much everyone will fill in instantly, number 9 Gareth Edwards and number 13 Phillipe Sella. That for me is the ultimate compliment I can offer "Monsieur Agen."

I wrote this chapter during the Covid-19 pandemic of 2020. On 15th January of that year, Phillipe Sella was placed on a ventilator at an Agen hospital.

He had been out enjoying a meal when he suddenly collapsed. "I thought I had had a heart attack" he explains. "I had chest pains and I was taken to the emergency room at the Clinique Saint-Hilaire where I lost consciousness.

"After some tests were carried out they discovered that my heart was fine but my lungs were infected. I spent two days in emergency care and five days in hospital. I don't know if it was Coronavirus. They told me I had pneumonia and it took me a while to recover. I had to stay flat for several weeks with antibiotics."

As the pandemic continued Phillipe resigned himself to isolation. "My mother is in Bourran and my dad is in a retirement home in Aiguillon so I have to respect the imposed lockdown.

"My family make fun of me at the moment because I send lots of pictures of birds from my garden. My wife Josey and I have never had so much time together, this is the good side of things."

It seems that infections and viruses are the one of the few things that can stop Phillipe Sella in his tracks but I'm happy to report that he is now back to full health and has resumed his essential role as "Mr Agen."

Chapter 14

Aurélien Rougerie
"The French will always be the French, that's the good news and the bad news."
Anon

It is a warm clear May night in the Auverne, the clock is reaching towards 9 p.m. at the Stade Marcel-Michelin, the home of ASM Clermont-Auvergne.

Standing in the centre of the pitch is Aurélien Rougerie, once described as "the Frenchest man in French rugby." He is misty-eyed with prototypical good looks, square jaw and flowing blond hair. He resembles a Parthenon sculpture more than a rugby player. With him are his three children huddled close to their father as the capacity home crowd roar their appreciation.

To his right, a massive homemade banner stretches across one of the stands. It reads:

"Merci Monsieur Rougerie."

After 19 seasons, and a staggering 417 appearances in the yellow and blue, this is "Roro's" final game for Clermont having been with them since the age of six when he started at ASM rugby school.

Nineteen years at the club with one of the longest names in the game, Montferrandaise Clermont Auvergne, is quite an achievement.

The date is 5th May 2018 and Toulouse have just been defeated 36-26 at the home of Association Sportive Montferrandaise Clermont Auverne to give them their full name, and for one last time Rougerie is leaving the field of play. This time it's to a guard of honour from both teams.

Substituted in the 53rd minute of the match, he has already completed his active service receiving a standing ovation from the 18,000 crowd as he made his way to the touchline.

Finally, with all the tributes over, Rougerie is carried off the field shoulder-high by teammates Wesley Fofana and Damien Penaud, two wonderful French international backs.

"I thought I would stop at the age of 33" says Rougerie. "I thought of leaving Clermont a couple of times in 2005 when the team was struggling and in 2013 when I got a lucrative offer from Japan by Toshiba Brave Lupus Tokyo. But the nuclear accident at the Fukushima plant put me off."

If Phillipe Sella was "Mr Agen" then there is no doubt that Aurélien Rougerie really earned the "Monsieur Clermont" tag.

Aurélien got the right-wing berth in this French XV for his raw power, strength and pace. At the top of his game he was a magnificent sight to behold.

When he first began to make an impact on French rugby, many in the media gave him the nickname "Le Lomu blanc." That may have been a slight exaggeration but to even be likened to the great Jonah is enough of a compliment on its own.

The world-famous tyre manufacturers, Michelin, designed, developed, patented and commercialized the radial tyre in Montferrand, and employed over 30,000 people locally.

The name is synonymous with the town and the rugby team so if we use some tyre analogies, Rougerie had serious "wheels" but would have probably required "slicks" and not radials with his blistering pace.

As with most of the French hard men in this book, he was not averse to indulging in the dark arts from time to time, a penchant he displayed in the Rugby World Cup Final of 2011 when France faced hosts New Zealand.

Perhaps having been born within spitting distance of the dormant volcano, the Puy de Dôme, in the commune of Beaumont, had an influence on Rougerie?

The huge wing created his own seismic activity every time he pounded down the right wing; he was an absolute beast and unlike his volcanic neighbour, he was always ready to erupt.

In the 2011 Rugby World Cup Final, Rougerie appeared to resurrect the ancient French combination of eye and head assault.

All Blacks captain Richie McCaw was the recipient of an alleged head butt and raking eye gouge courtesy of the blond winger. The incident was not picked up by the citing officer and McCaw did not complain, but a few days after the final, some video footage came to light showing McCaw on the floor. His reaction to referee Craig Joubert and the redness in his eye showed that something had occurred. As the evidence was not unearthed until three days after the match, it was outside the 36-hour citing window so no action could be taken.

Also in 2011, while captain of Clermont, he was cited after a particularly bad-tempered match against Toulon during which Cudmore and Malzieu received yellow cards along with Toulon's Genevois.

Rougerie was not only capable of dishing it out, he was also the victim on a couple of occasions both on and off the field.

In July 2014 while walking back to the team hotel in Millau during a pre-season training camp, Rougerie, along with team mates Julien Pierre and Benjamin Kayser, was attacked by armed men carrying machetes and swords. Some of the assailants were on scooters, and a court in Rodez to the north of Toulouse subsequently heard that the incident arose after a verbal altercation outside a night club. It was alleged that Rougerie confronted a man who had "insulted a woman" inside the building.

Rougerie is also no stranger to injury on the field, a notable incident occurring in a pre-season friendly in 2002 when Clermont faced Wasps. In the first minute of the match, Wasps hooker Phil Greening carried the ball and attempted to hand-off Rougerie. Play carried on and the referee saw nothing untoward.

However, the incident resulted in an injury to Rougerie's throat that resulted in him being hospitalized for 12 weeks, obliged to get his nutrition through a straw and having to undergo three operations on his windpipe. An abscess following the operation complicated matters further.

Rougerie sued Greening for loss of earnings in the French Civil Courts and claimed damages.

Greening knew nothing of the incident until after the final whistle when he was informed that Rougerie was in a bad way as a result of his hand-off.

On 16th November 2007, a court awarded Rougerie €90,000, ruling that Greening had fouled Rougerie "both technically and against the spirit of the game."

Phil Greening was convinced he had done nothing wrong, but the courts saw otherwise.

The Professional Rugby Players Association CEO, Damian Hopley, said: "This is very shocking for the game and sets a very dangerous precedent in a full-contact sport. Because of that, there is bound to be widespread concern at this ruling. Having seen the incident, it was a very straight forward case of a hand-off."

Rougerie's lawyer Jean-Paul Brousse said: "There is a price for pain, a price for the scar on Aurélien's neck and a price for loss of earnings."

So what made Rougerie such a magnificent physical specimen? Perhaps at least some of it is down to the DNA mix of his parents.

Father, Jacques, was known as "The Cube." He was a prop who played for Clermont and also on one occasion for France against Japan in 1973. Mother, Christine née Dulac, was a star basketball player who played 100 times for France as a shooting guard. She also had a spell as a local politician. Their boy, at 6ft 4in and 16 and a half stone, has undoubtedly inherited some top-flight sporting genes.

In the first half of the 2005 Six Nations match against Wales, in Paris, he provided us with a showcase of all his talents. Taking the ball as first receiver at centre as well as on his allocated right wing, he bullied and jostled while showing a desire to get the ball in his hands that was insatiable. Wales wing Shane Williams had a torrid time defending the blond tide that swept his way.

Shane reflects: "I gave Rougerie far too much time and space in the first half. He had an incredible 40 minutes. In the second half though it all changed and I ran rings around him!"

The fact that Wales made one of the greatest comebacks of all time in the second half to win the match should not detract from Rougerie's majestic first-half display.

In fact, he always seemed to produce that little bit extra when he was up against the men in red.

In Cardiff during the 2002 Six Nations he gave a stand-out performance, scoring his first international try and setting one up for centre Tony Marsh in a 33-37 win over Wales.

Rougerie made his international debut for France at the tender age of 21 against South Africa in 2001.

France coach Bernard Laporte thought Rougerie was the best thing since sliced baguettes, then subsequently dropped him abruptly after the semi-final defeat to England at the 2003 Rugby World Cup.

In 2008, when Marc Lièvremont succeeded Laporte as national coach, Rougerie was recalled to international duty.

His international career spanned 76 caps which involved 23 tries, two Grand Slams and a Rugby World Cup Final in 2011.

He has a 100-percent winning record as captain of France although that statistic is not as glorious as it seems. Rougerie was only captain for the one match, against Canada in the 2011 Rugby World Cup, a game won by France 46-19.

Rougerie was sometimes criticized for his defence but his courage was never in question and was amply demonstrated in February 2010 during the Six Nations match against Scotland at Murrayfield when he made quite an impact in the opening five minutes.

He managed to put in two huge hits, injuring himself in the process, which ruled him out of the following game against Ireland.

The Clermont wing hadn't played for his country for two years so he was clearly pumped up as he chased the kick-off and timed a massive hit on Kelly Brown perfectly. Unfortunately, Rougerie came off worse, needing treatment on his arm and shoulder before soldiering on.

Undeterred, a minute or so later he flew into another Scottish player, doing yet more damage to himself. The kamikaze winger took the full impact of Johnnie Beattie's shoulder to the jaw in a horrible-looking collision that effectively ended his match. He did stay on for a minute or so but when the ball came to him out wide, he dropped it and threw in the towel less than five minutes into the game.

It had been a long wait for him to get back into the French side, and sadly for him, two big collisions in the space of a few minutes ended his reappearance.

Aurélien's final international appearance for France came on 4th February 2012 at Stade de France where the home team defeated Italy 30-12.

The match was the first time new coach Philippe Saint-Andre was in charge. Early in the first period, scrum-half Dimitri Yachvili moved the ball out to Rougerie who found himself up against two Italian front-row forwards. It was no contest as he cut through to score his 23rd Test try. The score paved the way for a French victory.

In the autumn of 2018, on the day Clermont faced Toulon in the Top 14, a statue was unveiled outside Clermont's ground. It shows a man carrying the Bouclier de Brennus, the huge shield that is presented annually to the winners of the Top 14.

The statue is not engraved with a particular player's name but it is unmistakably Aurélien Rougerie.

It was Rougerie himself who modelled for the statue but this humble man would not let it bear his name. "I refused because there a lot of players who played this game at Clermont, and it's true in rugby that without the others we are not much."

The sculpture weighs more than seven tons and was paid for by Isidore Fartaria, owner of local company Labo France which supplies chemical products to serve the building sector.

When Bernard Laporte was the coach of France, he singled Rougerie out as a special player and described him as "The French horse."

There is no doubt the big winger was a thoroughbred and to see him thundering down the wing with his blond mane flowing was a joyous sight.

Had he been born with an extra pair of legs, I have no doubt he would have graced Longchamp with equal style and elegance.

It was rugby's good fortune to have ended up with the biped version for which we will all be eternally grateful.

Whether at wing or centre, when you saw Rougerie in the opposition ranks you knew you were in for a busy 80 minutes. He could hit you head-on like a runaway train or put on the after burners and take you on the outside. Either way you were in for a rough ride.

After retiring from the game, he opened up a complex in Clermont called HPark by Aurélien Rougerie, a 300 metre-square leisure complex consisting of squash courts, an indoor rugby pitch and a bar-brasserie which, according to the promotional material, provides "emotion, gluttony and conviviality around the values of rugby that we live in the Auvergne."

I guess some things get lost in translation (relish for or appreciation of food is a more nuanced meaning) but if gluttony is your thing then the brasserie can provide you with that good old fashioned French dish, fish and chips, for just under €14 which you can wash down with a beautiful Saint-Émilion Grand Cru but I have to advise that you will need your credit card for that one.

On the subject of gluttony, I wonder how many of the Seven Deadly Sins my 15 players here have committed. It's not a totting-up exercise I'm going to do. I respect these men but I also respect their lawyers!

On the walls of the establishment is another piece of homespun philosophy by the man from chapter six here, Jean-Pierre Rives.

"Rugby is the story of the ball with friends around and when there is no ball there are still friends." It is not one of J. P's greatest hits, but we get the sentiment.

Going back to that starry warm May night in 2018, as Aurélien Rougerie finally left Stade Marcel-Michelin for the last time as a player, he have might well have reflected on the words of another famous blond/blonde, Marilyn Monroe.

"Nothing lasts forever, so live it up, drink it down, laugh it off, avoid the drama. Take chances and never have regrets because at one point everything you did was exactly what you wanted."

Chapter 15

Émile Ntamack
"When you're down on the ground and you start thinking about your wife and children it means it's time to stop."
Pieter de Villiers

When it comes to rugby hard men, French full-backs have not been found to be out and out fighters. Many have proved wanting in the bravery stakes; in a lot of cases even the last-ditch tackle proved to be a step too far for them.

I've lost count of the number of times I've seen that thin blue line part (like a blue equivalent of the Red Sea in Exodus) and usher the try-scorer through as if a matador were guiding the way with his cape. Skulduggery was pretty much beyond the pay grade of French full-backs unless of course they were encouraged by a big forward who remained nearby to protect them.

Poitrenaud, Garbajosa, Jeanjean and Traille are just four names in a long cast list who have all had their maître d' moments. "Welcome to the try line sir!"

The greatest French full-back of all time, Serge Blanco, summed up the French full-back philosophy. "Rugby is just like love, you have to give before you can take, and when you have the ball it's like making love – you must think of the other's pleasure before your own." I'm pretty sure Serge didn't share his philosophy very loudly with Messrs Cholley and Ondarts.

There is one player, however, Émile "Milou" Ntamack who managed to provide a bit of physicality along with the pretty stuff. I never once saw him shirk a tackle so I was more than happy to award him the full-back role in my team.

Ntamack played full-back, wing and centre for France. On one occasion against Scotland in Paris during the 1999

Five Nations match, he played all three positions in one game! During the 46 matches he played for France, he wore the number 15 shirt five times so only just managed to reach the qualification standards although it has to said that my selection qualification standards are flexible.

The date is 3rd July 1994, the venue Eden Park, Auckland, home of the All Blacks and the one place where defeat is unthinkable.

France are facing New Zealand. There are 90 seconds left on the clock with the All Blacks leading 20-16.

In this two-match international Test series France have already beaten New Zealand in the first Test in Christchurch 8-22 and the All Blacks are desperate to level the series.

Fly-half Steve Bachop, attempting to run down the clock, kicks for touch from inside his own half but the kick doesn't find touch and Philippe Saint-André gathers the ball near the touchline inside his own "22". He turns to run it back with only seconds of the game remaining. Beating three defenders, he reaches the 10-metre line, Saint Andre is tackled and a ruck forms. Hooker Gonzales plays scrum-half at the ruck and feeds fly-half Deylaud, who in turn passes to Benazzi. Lurking on his right shoulder is The Black Panther, Émile Ntamack, his elegant loping stride barely touching the turf as he side-steps inside and gives the ball to Cabannes who runs right but passes left to the oncoming Deylaud. The fly-half steps inside a desperate All Black tackle inside the "22" and he passes left to Accoceberry.

New Zealand full-back John Timu comes racing across to tackle Accoceberry five metres from the goal line. Despite the tackle, Accoceberry manages to get his pass away to Jean-Luc Sadourny and the French full-back slides over to the left of the posts for a try that wins the match and the series. It's the first time a northern hemisphere team has won a Test series in The Land of the Long White Cloud.

The 44,000 crowd at Eden Park are stunned in disbelief.

It's one of the greatest tries of all time and known throughout the rugby world as "L'essai du bout du monde", the "Try from the End of the World."

The move lasted 65 seconds, spanned 80 metres and went through nine pairs of French hands.

The referee that day was Derek Bevan of Wales. After he awarded that try, as Sean Fitzpatrick trudged dejectedly behind the posts, Bevan turned to him and said: "What a wonderful try that was!" Fitzpatrick replied with two words, the first of which related to sex and the second concerned direction of motion.

The fact that Émile Ntamack was involved in such an historic running move comes as no surprise. The man from Lyon, born to a Cameroonian father and French mother, was one of the most beautiful runners the world game has produced.

He was one of the first black players to wear the blue jersey of France. There had been one or two previously but Ntamack was the pathfinder who modern-day black players followed.

Cameroon is in West Africa. From North Africa, Abdelatif Benazzi played for Morocco and France, while old and new prop idols Rabah Slimani and Mohamed Houras hailed from Algeria.

Mali ancestry produced Teddy Thomas, Wesley Fofana and Yacouba Camara, while Senegal provided Gaël Fickou and Djibril Camara.

More black players followed in the form of props Dany Priso from Cameroon, Demba Bamba from Mauritius and the wonderful flanker and captain, Thierry Dusautoir from the Ivory Coast.

The global reach of the French team saw the net being cast to Burkina Faso's Fulgence Ouedraogo, Yannick Nyanga from Zaire and Jimmy Marlu from Martinique. When you add the never-ending list of Fijians there is no doubt that French international rugby is now one heck of a cosmopolitan nation, and a lot of the credit for that goes to Emile Ntamack and Venezuela's Serge Blanco.

Lyon is a wonderful city with one foot in the town and one in the country. There is nothing more pleasurable than sitting at Cafe de la Place in Place Sathonay, a square in the 1st arrondissement at the bottom of La Croix-Rousse, one of the two hills of Lyon, enjoying a café gourmand.

A café gourmand is a many splendoured thing, a coffee that arrives at your table with three or four mini desserts.

The joy of going back and forth between the sweetness of the desserts and the bitterness of the coffee is a treat to the taste buds and one of life's great little pleasures.

But back to rugby. At first glance, Émile would not be considered particularly hard but at 6ft 3in and 14 and a half stone, there was an awful lot of boney, sinewy material to make big dents in defence and attack. He supplemented this with an abundance of bravery.

When starting his rugby career he was tall and lanky but not very tough. Émile worked tirelessly to fill out and managed to achieve some bulk without losing any of his dazzling speed.

The sporting genes in the Ntamack family are impressive. Brother Frank was capped by France against South Africa at number eight in 2001, this being his one and only appearance. His father was a weightlifter and soccer referee, his son Romain, a fly-half, is a star for Toulouse and France, and his other son Theo is also a member of the Toulouse squad.

"I played football and athletics" says Émile. "But I fell in love with rugby not just for the game itself but for its values."

You could see when Émile Ntamack was in full stride just how effortless and stylish he looked. He maintained beautiful form when he ran, and like Ed Moses the great

400-metre hurdler, he appeared to eat up the ground as he accelerated.

His nickname "The Black Panther" summed him up perfectly, just like the big cat. He was incredibly agile and had breath-taking speed.

The four-legged version can run at speeds of up to 35 mph, and having watched Emile in his pomp, I think his speedometer was not too far behind.

Ntamack's pace and shrewd reading of the game allowed him to become a master of the interception, as shown with the tries he scored against Ireland, Scotland and England at the 1995 Rugby World Cup as well as five years later in Cardiff. It was his signature dish, his speciality, once he had that ball in his hands and turned on the after burners there was no catching him.

When he arrived at Toulouse aged 18 he was given the nickname of "Snowy." This was not very original admittedly, but these were different times when PC referred only to computers and not political correctness.

He scored 21 tries in 49 European Cup matches for Stade Toulousain and was captain of the team that won the inaugural European Cup against Cardiff at the National Stadium in 1996.

"It was a memorable career highlight, time has passed but it is still engraved in my memory. I recall the Arms Park, a real temple of rugby, and an impressive Cardiff team who we only beat in extra time."

His international debut came in 1994 against Wales in Cardiff, a rare defeat for the French in those days, and on that particular afternoon it was another winger who stole the headlines, former Olympic hurdler, Nigel Walker of Wales, who showed his athletic prowess by racing in from 30 metres to score the winning try.

Émile played 46 times for France appearing on the winning side 32 times while losing 14 matches. Along the way, he scored 135 international points comprising 26 tries and the bonus of a conversion and a penalty against Ireland at Lansdowne Road in 1995.

His final home try for France came in one of the most entertaining Six Nations games of all time when Wales beat France at Stade de France in 1999. Emile scored a hat trick that day yet still ended up on the losing side.

His elusive running style was exemplified in the 2000 Six Nations where he made 13 clean breaks and beat 26 defenders.

Another remarkable fact is that he was on the winning side four times for France against the All Blacks. Not many players have that on their curriculum vitae, yet Ntamack was victorious in 1994 (twice), 1995 and 1999. He also holds a Rugby World Cup record for the most defenders beaten (45) and the most clean breaks (21).

Defences found Ntamack hard to catch, indeed the only thing that really slowed the Black Panther down was the curse of the athlete, injuries.

In January 1997 he was the victim of pubalgia, a strain of soft tissue in the groin that can turn into a hernia. It is an injury caused by twisting and turning running motions and kept Ntamack out of action until November 1998.

In 2001 he was the victim of serious injury during the match between Toulouse and Clermont. He suffered multiple fractures to the nose, eye and skull, and underwent a painful three-hour operation.

After Toulouse beat Perpignan in the 2003 Heineken Cup Final in Dublin, Ntamack announced his retirement from the game. "When we beat Perpignan in that final in Ireland I said that was it. I felt my career had come full circle" says Ntamack. "There was nothing more I could ask for after winning a second European Cup."

However, he had a change of heart and played on for one more season which ended with another European Cup final at Twickenham where Wasps beat Toulouse 27-20. Following that defeat, the retirement became official.

Ntamack had a pretty impressive record in finals. Apart from that defeat by Wasps, he won two European Finals in 1996 and 2003, six Top 14 Finals in 1994, 1995, 1996, 1997, 1999 and 2001, and the French Cup (Challenge Yves du Manoir) in 1993 and 1995.

After hanging up his boots, he moved into coaching with the Toulouse Under 21 team. International duty followed in 2005 when he took charge of the backs in the France Under 21 squad. A year later, *Les Bleus* were crowned world champions.

Global success propelled Ntamack into the national team camp in 2007. As a specialist coach of backs, he helped guide France to the Rugby World Cup final in 2011 where they lost narrowly to hosts, New Zealand 8-7.

Two seasons followed as coach with Bordeaux before a move back to his spiritual home and an appointment as Toulouse sporting director along with being coach of the club's youth teams.

The passage of time catches up with each and every one of us. Nothing brings this into sharp focus more than seeing the sons of the players you watched in your youth now taking their place on the international rugby stage.

As I am now into my early sixties I have seen Adam Hastings take over from Gavin, Damian Penaud from Alain and I've seen so many Quinnells and Moriartys for Wales that I have now lost count.

Romain and Emile Ntamack obviously fall into this category and their DNA seems to have a particular gene that becomes a lot more active once they set foot in Wales.

My theory is based on scientific evidence. Exhibit 'A' below is a case spanning 20 years based on two tries scored in Cardiff.

In 2020 Emile Ntamack intercepted a wayward pass from Shane Williams on the right wing and covered 40 meters unopposed to the try line to score against Wales in Cardiff.

In 2020, his son Romain intercepted a pass from Nick Tompkins in almost the identical spot and raced 70 metres without opposition to score a try against Wales in Cardiff. It was a wonderful moment for his father who finds watching his son play for *Les Bleus* much more nerve-racking and stressful than anything he endured during his career in the national team.

"I enjoy it when he [Romain] leaves the pitch while laughing. It is really tough and stressful watching, it's not just the possibility of injuries but also how good his choices are on the field. I wasn't nervous as a player but now I'm very stressed as a spectator."

Genetic memory, DNA or just sheer rugby beauty and talent. However you define it, Émile gets the number 15 shirt in my XV. Who knows? In 20 years' time someone might write a book similar to this one and son Romain's name might be included. By contrast, I'm not sure this author's genes are quite as durable as those of the brilliant rugby players who feature in the book.

One good thing, and there aren't too many, about being in my early sixties is the fact that I have had the pleasure, and the privilege, of watching some of the greatest runners that the game of rugby has produced.

From Gerald Davies, David Duckham and B. G. Williams to Cheslin Kolbe and Rieko Ioane via David Campese, Jason Robinson and Ieuan Evans, these greats of the game all had the one thing that you cannot legislate for and that is sheer pace. Some of them had jack-knife sidesteps, breath-taking outside swerves and bewildering change of pace. Emile Ntamack purred like an Aston Martin as he effortlessly shifted through the gears. He would have graced this illustrious company with his elegance, poise and his eye for the try line.

146

Epilogue

"Men are beasts, and even beasts don't behave as they do."
Brigitte Bardot

I thought long and hard about picking a bench for my French XV, an essential part of the modern professional game.

John Milton's poem summed up their role: "They also serve who only stand and wait," though in this case of course they would be sitting or doing stretching exercises.

I'm not even sure what you call those characters who inhabit the sidelines these days. For decades they were simply called replacements but thanks to the likes of Eddie Jones, they are now given the glamorous title of "Finishers" which is probably a more appropriate name for my bench as most of them have "finished" off quite a few of the opposition during their playing days.

For health and safety reasons I'm not going to allocate the shirts numbered 16 to 23 to any particular individuals. Specifically, this is for *my* health and safety!

There are a few frightening characters who are already not too impressed with my team selection so if I have to inform them they have missed out on a place on the bench as well, I might have to go into witness protection.

So, as an alternative, I will give you an overview of some of the names that raced through my cranium on those dark nights when I lay awake until the small hours ruminating about this book and its characters.

There were so many players that didn't make my Hard Men XV who were more than adequately qualified to do so. In fact I think it's fair to say that many of them were over qualified in terms of brute force.

Some of my early selections sadly turned down my requests for interviews and as a result they were instantly

147

dropped from the squad and subjected to disciplinary procedures. The results of those hearings will remain in-house.

The twin disciplinary panel consisted of myself and my black Labrador Rufus. We both sat in judgement in the kitchen with a Bonio and a cold glass of Guinness before arriving at our verdicts. Neither of us, it has to be said, showed any mercy.

I feel confident that my starting XV would give any team of any era a run for their money, and I would have loved to have seen them in the flesh and on the field of play.

Whichever of the "finishers" were awarded the shirts numbered 16-23, they would have certainly made an impact, quite literally in many cases.

Regarding the case of the front-row selections in particular, I was mining a rich seam.

To leave out Robert Paparemborde, Christian Califano, Pierre Dospital, Daniel Dubrocca, Vincent Moscato and Alain Paco, to name but a few, could leave me open to criminal prosecution the next time I venture down to the south of France.

Equally, the same could be said of the second row, where Fabien Pelous, Jean Condom, and Jean-François Imbernon were victims of my selection policy. As for Michel Palmié and Alain Estève, ("The Beast of Béziers"), I just hope they don't find out that I didn't select them or there will no doubt be a reception committee waiting to ambush me in a dark French alley as I amble away from a café crème establishment carrying only a copy of *L'Equipe* with which to defend myself.

The back row is another area the French have filled with distinction over the years, and my selections could be more than adequately shadowed by Laurent Rodriguez, Olivier Magne, Laurent Cabannes and Louis Picamoles, an amazing reservoir of talent that could fill a book on its own.

148

At scrum-half there was enough talent and hardness to fill the number nine shirt. What Pierre Berbizier and Jacques Fouroux lacked in height they made up for in attitude like little yappy dogs who think they are Alsatians. Those two bossed their forwards and bullied their opposite numbers in equal measure.

Another star candidate for the role was Jérôme Gallion who, in 1978, was rated second only to the great Gareth Edwards as the world's best scrum-half.

At fly-half Jean-Pierre Romeu and Alain Caussade were considered along with Gérald Merceron and Thierry Lacroix.

As for the backs, those glorious French backs, apart from the problem of locating a brave number 15, the centres and the wings have a rich and formidable undercard.

Jean-François Gourdon, the man who was on the receiving end of that famous J. P. R. shoulder barge that saved a Welsh Grand Slam, the "TGV" Patrick Estève, Éric Bonneval, the sadly departed Christophe Dominici and Vincent Clerc, were some of the wonderful wings I left out in the cold and if I could have found an ounce of hard man in him, then I would have given the full-back shirt to Serge Blanco in a heartbeat, one of the greatest rugby players I have ever seen.

Didier Codorniou, Roland Bertranne and Damien Traille were no soft centres in the chocolate box of rugby.

I know there will be plenty of discussion and disagreement with my selections, and that's just how it should be because debate and opinion are part of the wonderful tapestry of the glorious game that we love and cherish.

The breed of the true French rugby hard man is now virtually extinct but their spirit still lives on through glorious tales shared and enjoyed by rugby people over a beer, a glass of wine or a coffee.

I only hope this book has done them justice.

Allez Les Bleus!

People to thank

Without the donations of those listed below it would have been impossible for me to publish this book.

In such difficult times economically their generosity is even more wonderful.

Thank you each and every one of you from the bottom of my heart.

Emily Freeland (Barcelona)
Phil Steele (Equatorial Taffs Well)
Maryan Potart Raiss (Marignane)
Danny Daly (London)
Pascal Baker (Winchester/Aix)
Callum Chabal Baker
James Peak
Rémi Calandra (Stade Jean Bouin)
Elaine Jones (Wrexham/London)
Noel Kelleher
Tom Dickson (Toulouse/London)
Wendy Pearce (Poole)
Brenham Jones (Sydney, Australia)

Printed in Great Britain
by Amazon

12591311R00092